The Book of the Bee

Translated by

Earnest A. Wallis Budge

First published in 1886

Published by Left of Brain Books

Copyright © 2023 Left of Brain Books

ISBN 978-1-397-66809-7

First Edition

All rights reserved. No part of this publication may be reproduced, distributed, or transmitted in any form or by any means, including photocopying, recording, or other electronic or mechanical methods, without the prior written permission of the publisher, except in the case of brief quotations permitted by copyright law. Left of Brain Books is a division of Left Of Brain Onboarding Pty Ltd.

PUBLISHER'S PREFACE

About the Book

"The Book of the Bee is a Nestorian Christian sacred history. According to Budge it was written ca. A.D. 1222 by a Syrian bishop named Solomon (Shelêmôn). There is very little about the work itself in the Preface to this edition, it being concerned primarily with the manuscript sources. In the Introduction to the Book of the Cave of Treasures, Budge says that Solomon's object in writing the Book of the Bee was to present 'a full history of the Christian Dispensation according to the Nestorians.'"

(Quote from sacred-texts.com)

CONTENTS

PUBLISHER'S PREFACE
PREFACE 1
INTRODUCTION 6
  OF GOD'S ETERNAL INTENTION IN RESPECT OF THE CREATION OF THE
  UNIVERSE 11
  OF THE CREATION OF THE SEVEN NATURES (SUBSTANCES) IN SILENCE 12
  OF EARTH, WATER, AIR, AND FIRE 13
  OF HEAVEN 14
  OF THE ANGELS 15
  OF DARKNESS 18
  OF EFFUSED (CIRCUMAMBIENT) LIGHT 19
  OF THE FIRMAMENT 20
  OF THE CREATION OF TREES AND PLANTS, AND THE MAKING OF SEAS AND
  RIVERS 21
  OF THE MAKING OF THE LUMINARIES 22
  OF THE CREATION OF SEA-MONSTERS, FISH, WINGED FOWL, AND THE
  REPTILES THAT ARE IN THE SEAS 23
  OF THE CREATION OF BEASTS AND ANIMALS 24
  OF THE FORMATION OF ADAM 25
  OF THE MAKING OF EVE 26
  OF PARADISE 27
  OF THE SIN OF ADAM 29
  OF THE EXPULSION OF ADAM AND EVE FROM PARADISE 31
  OF ADAM'S KNOWING EVE 32
  OF THE INVENTION OF THE INSTRUMENTS FOR WORKING IN IRON ... 34
  OF NOAH AND THE FLOOD 35
  OF MELCHIZEDEK 38
  OF THE GENERATIONS OF NOAH 40
  OF THE SUCCESSION OF GENERATIONS FROM THE FLOOD UNTIL NOW 42
  OF THE BUILDING OF THE TOWER AND THE DIVISION OF TONGUES 44
  OF ABRAHAM 45
  OF THE TEMPTATION OF JOB 46
  OF THE BLESSINGS OF ISAAC 48
  OF JOSEPH 49
  OF MOSES AND THE CHILDREN OF ISRAEL 51
  THE HISTORY OF MOSES' ROD 53
  OF JOSHUA THE SON OF NUN, AND BRIEF NOTICES OF THE YEARS OF THE
  JUDGES AND THE KINGS OF THE CHILDREN OF ISRAEL 66
  OF THE DEATH OF THE PROPHETS; HOW THEY DIED, AND (WHERE) EACH
  ONE OF THEM WAS BURIED 68

- OF THE MESSIANIC GENERATIONS 72
- OF THE ANNUNCIATION OF THE ANGEL TO YÔNÂKÎR (JOACHIM) IN RESPECT OF MARY 74
- OF THE ANNUNCIATION BY GABRIEL TO MARY OF THE CONCEPTION OF OUR LORD 76
- OF THE BIRTH OF OUR LORD IN THE FLESH 78
- THE PROPHECY OF ZÂRÂDÔSHT CONCERNING OUR LORD 79
- OF THE STAR WHICH APPEARED IN THE EAST ON THE DAY OF THE BIRTH OF OUR LORD 81
- OF THE COMING OF THE MAGI FROM PERSIA 83
- OF OUR LORD'S GOING DOWN INTO EGYPT 85
- OF JOHN THE BAPTIST, AND OF THE BAPTISM OF OUR LORD 87
- OF OUR LORD'S FAST; OF THE STRIFE WHICH HE WAGED WITH THE DEVIL; AND OF THE MIGHTY DEEDS THAT HE WROUGHT 89
- OF THE PASSOVER OF OUR LORD 90
- OF THE PASSION OF OUR LORD 92
- OF THE RESURRECTION OF OUR LORD 96
- OF THE ASCENSION OF OUR LORD TO HEAVEN 97
- OF THE DESCENT OF THE HOLY SPIRIT UPON THE APOSTLES IN THE UPPER CHAMBER 99
- OF THE TEACHING OF THE APOSTLES, AND OF THE PLACES OF EACH ONE OF THEM, AND OF THEIR DEATHS 101
- THE NAMES OF THE APOSTLES IN ORDER 109
- OF SOME MINOR MATTERS 111
- THE NAMES OF THE EASTERN CATHOLICS, THE SUCCESSORS OF THE APOSTLES ADDAI AND MÂRÎ 112
- THE NAMES OF THE KINGS WHO HAVE REIGNED IN THE WORLD FROM THE FLOOD UNTIL NOW 117
- OF THE END OF TIMES AND THE CHANGE OF KINGDOMS; FROM THE BOOK OF METHODIUS, BISHOP OF ROME 122
- OF GOG AND MAGOG, WHO ARE IMPRISONED IN THE NORTH 125
- OF THE COMING OF THE ANTICHRIST, THE SON OF PERDITION 127
- OF DEATH AND THE DEPARTURE OF THE SOUL FROM THE BODY 129
- OF THE QUICKENING AND THE GENERAL RESURRECTION, THE CONSUMMATION OF THE MATERIAL WORLD AND THE BEGINNING OF THE NEW WORLD 131
- OF THE MANNER AND STATE IN WHICH MEN WILL RISE IN THE DAY OF THE RESURRECTION 134
- OF THE HAPPINESS OF THE RIGHTEOUS AND THE TORMENT OF SINNERS, AND IN WHAT STATE THEY ARE THERE 136
- WHETHER MERCY WILL BE SHEWN TO SINNERS AND THE DEVILS IN GEHENNA, AFTER THEY HAVE BEEN TORMENTED AND SUFFERED AND BEEN PUNISHED, OR NOT? AND IF MERCY IS TO BE SHEWN TO THEM, WHEN WILL IT BE 138
- ENDNOTES 141

PREFACE

OF the author of 'the Book of the Bee,' the bishop Shelêmôn or Solomon, but very little is known. He was a native of Khilât or Akhlât (in Armenia, at the western end of lake Vân), and by religious profession a Nestorian. He became metropolitan bishop of al-Basra (in al-`Irâk, on the right bank of the united streams of the Tigris and Euphrates) about A.D. 1222, in which year he was present at the consecration of the catholicus or Nestorian patriarch Sabr-îshô` (Hope-in-Jesus)[1] (see Assemânî, Bibl. Orient., t. ii, no. 75; Barhebraeus, Chron. Eccl., t. ii, p. 371). In the Catalogue of Ecclesiastical Works compiled by `Ebêd-yêshû` or `Abd-îshô` (the-Servant-of-Jesus) he is stated to have written, besides 'the Bee,' a treatise on the figure of the heavens and the earth, and sundry short discourses and prayers (see Assemânî, Bibl. Orient., t. iii, pt. i, where there is a lengthy analysis of the contents of 'the Bee'). A Latin translation of 'the Bee' by Dr. J. M. Schoenfelder appeared at Bamberg in 1866; it is based upon the Munich MS. only, and is faulty in many places.

The text of 'the Bee,' as contained in this volume, is edited from four MSS., indicated respectively by the letters A, B, C and D.

The MS. A[2] belongs to the Library of the Royal Asiatic Society of Great Britain and Ireland. It is dated A.Gr. 1880 = A.D. 1569, and consists of 188 paper leaves, measuring about 8 in. by 5¾. Each page is occupied by one column of writing, generally containing 25 lines. This MS. is so stained and damaged by water in parts that some of the writing is illegible. The quires are twenty-one in number and, excepting the last two, are signed with letters. Leaves are wanting after folios 6, 21, 49, 125, 166 and 172; and in several pages there are lacunae of one, two and more lines. The volume is written in a good Nestorian hand, with numerous vowel-points. Originally it was the property of the priest Wardâ, son of the deacon Moses, who was prior of the convent of Mâr Ezekiel. Later on, it belonged to one Mâr John of Enzelli (near Resht, on the south shore of the Caspian Sea). In the year A.Gr. 1916 = A.D. 1605 it was bound by a person whose name has been erased. The Book of the Bee occupies foll. 26 a to 92 b, and the colophon runs: 'By the help of our Lord and our God, this Book of the Bee was completed on the 16th day of the month of Tammuz, on the Saturday that ushers in the Sunday which is called Nûsârdêl[3], in the year 1880 of the blessed Greeks, by the hands of the sinful servant the faulty Elias. Amen.'

The MS. B is on paper, and is numbered Add. 25,875 in the British Museum. See Wright's Catal., p. 1064, no. dccccxxii, ff. 81 b-158 a. It is written in a good Nestorian hand, with numerous vowel-points, etc., and is dated A.Gr. 2020 = A.D. 1709. The colophon runs:--

'It was finished in the year 2020 of the Greeks, on Friday the 22nd of the blessed month Tammûz, by the wretched sinner, the deacon Hômô of Alkôsh[4]. I entreat you to pray for him that perchance he may obtain mercy with those upon whom mercy is freely shewn in the day of judgment, Amen. And to Jah be the glory, Amen.

'The illustrious priest and pure verger, the priest Joseph, the son of the late deacon Hormizd of Hôrdaphnê[5], took pains and was careful to have this book written: may Christ make his portion in the kingdom of heaven! Amen. He had it written for the holy church called after the name of our Lady Mary the pure and virgin mother, which is in the blessed and happy village of Hôrdaphnê in the district of `Amêdîa. From now and henceforth this book remains the property of the (above-) mentioned church, and no man shall have power over it to carry it off for any reprehensible cause of theft or robbery, or to give it away without the consent of its owners, or to abstract it and not to return it to its place. Whosoever shall do this, he shall be banned and cursed and execrated by the word of our Lord; and all corporeal and incorporeal beings shall say "Yea and Amen."'

From the manner in which B ends, it would seem either that the MS. from which it was copied was imperfect, or that the scribe Hômô omitted to transcribe the last leaf of the MS. before him, probably because it contained views on man's future state which did not coincide with his own.

The MS. C, belonging to the Royal Library at Munich, consists of 146 paper leaves, measuring about 12 1/8 in. by 8¼. There are two columns, of twenty-four lines each, to a page; the right-hand column is Syriac, the left Kârshûnî or Arabic in Syriac characters. The MS. is beautifully written in a fine Nestorian hand, and vowels and diacritical points have been added abundantly. The headings of the chapters are in Estrangelâ. The last two or three leaves have been torn out, and on fol. 147 a there are eighteen lines of Kârshûnî in another hand, which contain the equivalent in Arabic of B, fol. 157 a, col. 2, lines 10 to 24.

On the fly-leaf are five lines of Arabic, which run:--

'This book is the property of the church of Mâr Cyriacus the Martyr at Batnâye[6]. The deacon Peter bar Saumô has purchased it for the church with its own money, and therefore it has become the lawful property of the church. Whosoever taketh it away without the consent of the directors of the church, committeth sin and is bound to restore it. This was on the 17th of the month of Âdhâr in the year of our Lord 1839, in the protected city of Mosul.'

Dr. Schoenfelder in the preface to his translation, assigns this MS. to the fourteenth century ('ad saeculum decimum quartum procul dubio pertinet'). From this view, however, I differ for the following reasons. The MS. B, dated A.Gr. 2020 = A.D. 1709, is written upon water-lined paper, having for water-mark upon each leaf three crescents of different sizes, and a sign like a V:--

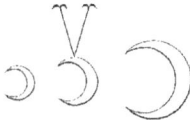

The paper is smooth and thick. The Munich MS. C is written upon rather rougher paper, but with the same water-mark exactly, only the three crescents are on one leaf, and the V-shaped mark upon that next to it. Therefore Dr. E. Maunde Thompson, keeper of the MSS. in the British Museum, who has kindly given me the benefit of his great experience in these matters, considers that the paper on which these two MSS. are written was made at the same manufactory and about the same time[7]. Add to this that the writing of both MSS. is almost identical, and that the signatures of the quires and the style of ornamentation is the same, and it will be evident that the Munich MS. belongs rather to the end of the seventeenth or the beginning of the eighteenth century than to the fourteenth[8].

The MS. D, belonging to the Bodleian Library, Oxford[9], consists of 405 paper leaves, measuring 8 5/8 in. by 6¼. There is one column of twenty-one lines, in Kârshûni or Arabic in Syriac characters, to each page. The MS. is written in a fine bold hand, the headings of the chapters, names, and diacritical points being in red. It is dated Friday the 28th day of Âb, A.Gr. 1895 = A.D. 1584, and was transcribed by Peter, the son of Jacob.

The Arabic version of 'the Bee' contained in this MS. borders at times on a very loose paraphrase of the work. The writer frequently repeats himself, and occasionally translates the same sentence twice, though in different words, as if to make sure that he has given what he considers to be the sense of the Syriac. He adds paragraphs which have no equivalents in the three Syriac copies of 'the Bee' to which I have had access, and he quotes largely from the Old and New Testaments in support of the opinions of Solomon of Basrah. The order of the chapters is different, and the headings of the different sections into which the chapters are divided will be found in the selections from the Arabic versions of 'the Bee'. This MS. is of the utmost importance for the study of 'the Bee,' as it contains the last chapter in a perfect and complete state; which is unfortunately not the case either with the bilingual Munich MS. or the copy in Paris[10].

Assemânî says in the Bibl. Orient., t. iii, pt. i, note 4, that there are two codices of 'the Bee' in the Vatican Library, and he has described them in his great work--MSS. Codicum Bibliothecae Apostol. Vatic. Catalogus, t. iii, nos. clxxvi and clxxvii. The latter is incomplete, containing only forty chapters (see Bibl. Orient., t. ii, p. 488, no. ix); but the former is complete (see Bibl. Orient., t. i, p. 576, no. xvii). It was finished, according to a note at the end, on Wednesday, 14th of Shebât in the year of Alexander, the son of Nectanebus[11], 1187, which Assemânî corrects into 1787 = A.D. 1476. The name of the scribe was Gabriel, and he wrote it for the 'priest John, son of the priest Jonah' (Yaunân), living at the village of ### in the district of Baz, (see Hoffmann, Auszüge aus syr. Akten pers. Martyrer, pp. 204-5). At a subsequent time it belonged to the church of Mâr Cyriacus in the village of Sâlekh, in the district of Barwar, (see Hoffmann, op. cit., pp. 193, 204).

My translation aims at being literal, and will, I hope, be found more correct in some places than that of Dr. Schoenfelder. I have added brief notes only where it seemed absolutely necessary. A few Syriac words, which are either wanting or not sufficiently explained in Castell-Michaelis's Lexicon, have been collected in a 'Glossary,' on the plan of that in Wright's Kal⁻ilah and Dimnah. The Index will probably be useful to the English reader. {The glossary and index are not included in this version.}

My thanks are due to Mr. E. B. Nicholson and Dr. A. Neubauer of the Bodleian Library, to the authorities of the Royal Library at Munich, and to the late W. S. W. Vaux, Secretary of the Royal Asiatic Society, for the loan of the MSS. of 'the Bee' preserved in their respective collections. Professor Wright has edited the extracts from the Arabic versions of 'the Bee,' and read a proof of each sheet of the whole book from first to last, besides giving me much general help and guidance in the course of my work. I dedicate this book to him as a mark of gratitude for a series of kindnesses shewn to me during the past nine years.

E. A. WALLIS BUDGE.

LONDON,
October 23, 1886.

INTRODUCTION

TRUSTING in the power of our Lord Jesus Christ, we begin to write this book of gleanings called 'The Bee,' which was composed by the saint of God, Mâr Solomon, metropolitan of Perath-Maishân[12], that is Bassorah (al-Basrah), one of His companions. O Lord, in Thy mercy help me. Amen.

FIRST, THE APOLOGY

'The children ought not to lay up treasures for the parents, but the parents for the spiritual children,' saith the blessed Paul[13]; therefore we are bound to repay thee the debt of love, O beloved brother and staff of our old age, saint of God, Mâr Narses[14], bishop of Khônî-Shâbôr Bêth-Wâzik[15]. We remember thy solicitude for us, and thy zeal for our service, which thou didst fulfil with fervent love and Christ-like humility. And when we had loving meetings with each other from time to time, thou wert wont to ask questions and to make enquiries about the various things which God hath wrought in His dispensation in this material world, and also as to the things that He is about to do in the world of light. But since we were afflicted with the Mosaic defect of hesitancy of speech, we were unable to inform thee fully concerning the profitable matters about which, as was right, thou didst enquire; and for this reason we were prevented from profitable discourse upon the holy Books. Since, then, God has willed and ruled our separation from each other, and the sign of old age, which is the messenger of death, hath appeared in us, and we have grown old and come into years, it has seemed good to us, with the reed for a tongue and with ink for lips, to inform thee briefly concerning God's dispensation in the two worlds. And, behold, we have gleaned and collected and gathered together chapters and sections relating to this whole universe from the garden of the divine Books and from the crumbs of the Fathers and the Doctors, having laid down as the foundation of our building the beginning of the creation of this world, and concluding with the consummation of the world to come. We have called this book the 'Book of the Bee,' because we have gathered of the blossoms of the two Testaments and of the flowers of the holy Books, and have placed them therein for thy benefit. As the common bee with gauzy wings flies about, and flutters over and lights upon flowers of various colours, and upon blossoms of divers odours, selecting and gathering from all of them the materials which are useful for the construction of her handiwork; and having first of all collected the materials from the flowers, carries them upon her thighs, and bringing them to her dwelling, lays a foundation for her building with a base of wax; then gathering in her mouth some of the heavenly dew which is upon the blossoms of spring, brings it and blows it into these cells; and weaves the comb and honey for the use of men and her own nourishment: in like manner have we, the infirm, hewn the stones of corporeal words from the rocks of the Scriptures which are in the Old Testament, and have laid them down as a foundation for the edifice of the spiritual law. And as the bee carries the waxen substance upon her thighs because of its insipidity and tastelessness, and brings the honey in her mouth because of its sweetness and value; so also have we laid down the corporeal law by way of substratum and foundation, and the spiritual law for a roof and ceiling to the edifice of the spiritual tower. And as the expert gardener and orchard-keeper goes round among the gardens, and seeking out the finest sorts of fruits takes from them slips and shoots, and plants them in his own field; so also have we gone into the garden of the divine Books, and have culled therefrom branches and shoots, and have planted them in the ground of this book for thy consolation and benefit. When thou, O brother, art recreating thyself among these plants, those which appear and which thou dost consider to be insipid and tasteless, leave for thy companions, for they may be more suitable to others (than to thee); but, upon those which are sweet, and which sweeten the palate of thy understanding, do thou feed and satisfy thy hunger. If, however, owing to their fewness, they do not fill thee, seek in succession for their roots, and from thence shall thy want be satisfied. Know also, O brother, that where there is true love, there is no fear[16]; and where there is freedom of speech, there is no dread; and we should not dare to be so rash as to enter upon these subjects, which are beyond the capacity of our simple understanding, unless we relied upon thy immaculate love; because, in the words of one of the inspired[17], 'When thou findest honey, eat (only) so much as is sufficient for thee, lest, when thou art sated, thou vomit it[18]'; that is to say, do not enquire (too closely) into the divine words.

LIST OF THE CHAPTERS IN THIS BOOK

I. Of God's eternal intention in respect of the creation of the universe.
II. Of the creation of the seven natures (substances) in silence.

III. Of earth, water, air, and fire.
IV. Of heaven.
V. Of the angels.
VI. Of darkness.
VII. Of effused (circumambient) light.
VIII. Of the firmament.
IX. Of the creation of trees and plants, and the making of seas and rivers.
X. Of the making of the luminaries.
XI. Of the creation of sea-monsters, fish, winged fowl, and the reptiles that are in the seas.
XII. Of the creation of beasts and animals.
XIII. Of the formation of Adam.
XIV. Of the making of Eve.
XV. Of Paradise.
XVI. Of the sin of Adam.
XVII. Of the expulsion of Adam and Eve from Paradise.
XVIII. Of Adam's knowing Eve.
XIX. Of the invention of the instruments for working in iron.
XX. Of Noah and the Flood.
XXI. Of Melchizedek.
XXII. Of the generations of Noah, how seventy-two families sprang from three sons.
XXIII. Of the succession of generations from the Flood until now.
XXIV. Of the building of the Tower.
XXV. Of Abraham.
XXVI. Of the temptation of Job.
XXVII. Of Isaac's blessing upon Jacob.
XXVIII. Of Joseph.
XXIX. Of Moses and the Children of Israel.
XXX. Of Moses' rod.
XXXI. Of Joshua the son of Nun, and the Judges, and brief notices of the Kings of the Children of Israel.
XXXII. Of the death of the Prophets; how they died, and (where) they were buried.
XXXIII. Of the divine dispensation which was wrought in the New Testament, and of the genealogy of Christ.
XXXIV. Of the announcement of the angel to Jonachir (Joachim) in respect of Mary.
XXXV. Of the annunciation of Gabriel to Mary in respect of her conception of our Lord.

XXXVI. Of our Lord's birth in the flesh.
XXXVII. Of the prophecy of Zarâdôsht, that is Baruch the scribe.
XXXVIII. Of the star which appeared in the East on the day of our Lord's birth.
XXXIX. Of the coming of the Magi from Persia, and the slaughter of the infants.
XL. Of the going down of our Lord into Egypt.
XLI. Of John the Baptist and his baptism of our Lord.
XLII. Of our Lord's fast and His contest with Satan.
XLIII. Of the passover of our Lord.
XLIV. Of the passion of our Lord.
XLV. Of the resurrection of our Lord.
XLVI. Of the ascension of our Lord.
XLVII. Of the descent of the Holy Ghost upon the Apostles in the upper chamber.
XLVIII. Of the teaching of the Apostles, their deaths, and the place where each of them (was buried).
XLIX. The names of the twelve Apostles and the seventy (Disciples), one after another in (his) grade.
L. Of minor matters; those of the Apostles who were married, etc.
LI. The names of the Eastern Patriarchs, and the places where they were buried[19].
LII. The names of the kings who have reigned in the world from the Flood to the present time, and the (number of the) years of the reign of each of them. The names of the kings of the Medes and the Egyptians; the names of the seventy old men who brought out the Scriptures and translated them; the names of the Roman emperors, and of the kings of Persia.
LIII. Of the end of times and the change of kingdoms. From the book of Methodius, the bishop of Rome.
LIV. Of Gog and Magog, who are imprisoned in the North.
LV. Of the coming of Antichrist, the son of perdition.
LVI. Of death and the departure of the soul from the body.
LVII. Of the rising of the dead and the general resurrection, the end of the material world, and the beginning of the new world.
LVIII. Of the manner in which men will rise in the day of the resurrection.
LIX. Of the happiness of the righteous, and the torture of sinners; and of the manner in which they will exist yonder.
LX. Of the demons and sinners in Gehenna, whether after they have been punished and have suffered and received their sentence, they will have

mercy shewn to them or not; and if mercy be shewn to them, when it will be.

OF GOD'S ETERNAL INTENTION IN RESPECT OF THE CREATION OF THE UNIVERSE

IT is well for us to take the materials for our discourse from the divine Scriptures, that we may not stray from the straight paths of the way of truth. The blessed David saith, 'Lord, thou hast been our dwelling-place in all generations, before the mountains were conceived[20].' David, the harpist of the Spirit, makes known thereby, that although there was a beginning of the framing of Adam and the other creatures when they were made, yet in the mind of God it had no beginning; that it might not be thought that God has a new thought in respect of anything that is renewed day by day, or that the construction of Creation was newly planned in the mind of God: but everything that He has created and is about to create, even the marvellous construction of the world to come, has been planned from everlasting in the immutable mind of God. As the natural child in the womb of his mother knows not her who bears him, nor is conscious of his father, who, after God, is the cause of his formation; so also Adam, being in the mind of the Creator, knew Him not. And when he was created, and recognised himself as being created, he remained with this knowledge six hours only[21], and there came over him a change, from knowledge to ignorance and from good to evil. Hence, when Divine Providence wished to create the world, the framing of Adam was first designed and conceived in the mind of God, and then that of the (other) creatures; as David saith, 'Before the mountains were conceived.' Consequently, Adam is older than the (other) creatures in respect of his conception, and the (other) creatures are older than Adam in respect of their birth and their being made. And whereas God created all creatures in silence and by a word, He brought forth Adam out of His thoughts, and formed him with His holy hands, and breathed the breath of life into him from His Spirit, and Adam became a living soul[22], and God gave him the knowledge of the difference between good and evil. When he perceived his Creator, then was God formed and conceived within the mind of man; and man became a temple to God his maker, as it is written, 'Know ye not that ye are the temple of God, and that the Spirit of God dwelleth in you[23]?' And again, 'I will dwell in them, and walk in them[24].'

OF THE CREATION OF THE SEVEN NATURES (SUB-STANCES) IN SILENCE

WHEN God in His mercy wished to make known all His power and His wisdom, in the beginning, on the evening of the first day, which is Sunday, He created seven natures (substances) in silence, without voice. And because there was as yet none to hear a sound, He did well to create them in silence, that He might not make anything uselessly; but He willed, and heaven, earth, water, air, fire, and the angels and darkness, came into being from nothing.

OF EARTH, WATER, AIR, AND FIRE

THE earth was tôh we-bôh[25], that is to say, it was unarranged and unadorned, but plunged in the midst of the waters. The waters were above it, and above the waters was air, and above the air was fire. The earth is by nature cold and dry. Dry land appeared on the third day, when the trees and plants were created; and the waters were separated therefrom on the second day, when the firmament was made from them. Water is by nature cold and moist. As touching the 'Spirit which was brooding upon the face of the waters[26],' some men have ignorantly imagined it to have been the Holy Spirit[27], while others have more correctly thought it to have been this air (of ours). Air is by nature hot and moist. Fire was operating in the upper ether, above the atmosphere; it possessed heat only, and was without luminosity until the fourth day, when the luminaries were created: we shall mention it in the chapter on the luminaries (chap. x). Fire is by nature hot and dry.

OF HEAVEN

HEAVEN is like a roof to the material world, and will serve as the floor of the new world. It is by nature shining and glorious, and is the dwelling-place of the invisible hosts. When God spread out this firmament, He brought up above it a third part of the waters, and above these is the heaven of light and of the luminaries. Hence people say 'the heaven, and the heaven of heavens[28]'; for we call both the firmament and the waters which are above it 'heaven.' Some consider that the verse 'Let the waters which are above the heavens praise the name of the Lord[29]' refers to the holy angels and to our Lord's humanity; but neither the Church nor the orthodox teachers accept this.

OF THE ANGELS[30]

THE Angels consist of nine classes and three orders, upper, middle and lower. The upper order is composed of Cherubim, Seraphim, and Thrones: these are called 'priests' (kumrê), and 'chief priests,' and 'bearers of God's throne.' The middle order is composed of Lords, Powers and Rulers[31]: these are called 'priests' (kâhnê), because they receive revelations from those above them. The lower order consists of Principalities, Archangels and Angels: and these are the ministers who wait upon created things. The Cherubim are an intellectual motion[32] which bears the throne of the holy Trinity, and is the chief of all motions; they are ever watchful of the classes of themselves and those beneath them. As concerning the epithet 'full of eyes[33],' which is applied to them, the eyes indicate the mystery of the revelations of the Trinity. Their head, and the foremost and highest among them, is Gabriel, who is the mediator between God and His creation. The Seraphim are a fiery motion, which warms those below it with the fire of the divine love. The six wings which each of them is said to possess[34] indicate the revelations which they receive from the Creator and transmit to mankind. The Thrones are a fixed motion, which is not shaken by the trials which come upon it. The Lords are a motion which is entrusted with the government of the motions beneath it; and it is that which prevents the demons from injuring created things. The Powers are a mighty motion, the minister of the will of the Lord; and it is that which gives victory to some rulers in battle and defeat to others. The Rulers are a motion which has power over the spiritual treasures, to distribute them to its companions according to the will of the Creator. This class of angels governs the luminaries, the sun, moon, and stars. The Principalities are a defined motion which possesses the direction of the upper ether, of rain, clouds, lightning, thunder, whirlwinds, tempests, winds, and other ethereal disturbances. The Archangels are a swift operative motion, into whose hands is entrusted the government of the wild beasts, cattle, winged fowl, reptiles, and everything that hath life, from the gnat to the elephant, except man. The Angels are a motion which has spiritual knowledge of everything that is on earth and in heaven. With each and every one of us is an angel of this group--called the guardian angel--who directs man from his conception until the general resurrection.

The number of each one of these classes of angels is equal to the number of all mankind from Adam to the resurrection. Hence it is handed down that the number of people who are going to enter the world is equal to the number of all the heavenly hosts; but some say that the number is equal to that of one of the classes only, that they may fill the place of those of them who have fallen through transgressing the law; because the demons fell from three classes (of angels), from each class a third part. If then it is an acknowledged fact that there are three orders of angels, and in each order there are three classes, and in every class a number equivalent to that of all mankind, what is the total number of the angels? Some say that when the angels were created, and were arranged in six divisions--Cherubim, Seraphim, Thrones, Principalities, Archangels, and Angels--the three lower divisions reflected (saying), 'What is the reason that these are set above, and we below? for they have not previously done anything more than we, neither do we fall short of them.' On account of this reflection as a cause, according to the custom of the (divine) government, Justice took from both sides, and established three other middle classes of angels--Lords, Powers, and Rulers--that the upper might not be (unduly) exalted, nor the lower think themselves wronged. As for the dwelling-place of the angels, some say that above the firmament there are waters, and above them another heaven in the form of infinite light, and that this is the home of the angels. Here too is God without limit, and the angels, invisible to bodily eyes, surround the throne of His majesty, where they minister to 'the tabernacle not made with hands[35].' Others say that, from the beginning, when God created the angels, until the second day, in which the firmament was made, all the classes of angels dwelt in the upper heavens; but when the firmament was made, they all came down below it, with the exception of three classes--the Cherubim, Seraphim, and Thrones[36]--who remained above it. These surrounded and supported the Shechinah of God from the beginning of the world until our Lord ascended unto heaven; and after the Ascension, behold, they surround and support the throne of the Christ God, who is over all, until the end of the world. The Expositor[37] and his companions say: 'The tabernacle which Moses made is a type of the whole world.' The outer tabernacle is the likeness of this world, but the inner tabernacle is the similitude of the place that is[38] above the firmament. And as the priests ministered in the outer tabernacle daily, while the high priest alone entered into the inner tabernacle once a year; so of all rational beings, angels and men, no one has entered (the place) above the firmament, save the High Priest of our confession, Jesus Christ[39]. The fathers, when they have been deemed worthy at any time to see our Lord in a revelation, have seen Him in heaven, surrounded by the Cherubim and Seraphim. Hence some say that there are angels above the heavens. All these celestial hosts have revelations both of sight and of hearing; but the Cherubim have revelations by sight only, because there is no mediator between them and God. The angels have an intellect superior to that of the rest of rational beings; man has stronger desire, and the demons a greater degree of anger.

OF DARKNESS

DARKNESS is a self-existent nature; and if it had not had a nature, it would not have been reckoned among the seven natures which were created in the beginning in silence. Others say that darkness is not a self-existent nature, but that it is the shadow of bodies.

OF EFFUSED (CIRCUMAMBIENT) LIGHT

WHEN the holy angels were created on the evening of the first day, without voice, they understood not their creation, but thought within themselves that they were self-existent beings and not made. On the morning of the first day God said in an audible and commanding voice, 'Let there be light[40],' and immediately the effused light was created. When the angels saw the creation of light, they knew of a certainty that He who had made light had created them. And they shouted with a loud voice, and praised Him, and marvelled at His creation of light, as the blessed teacher[41] saith, 'When the Creator made that light, the angels marvelled thereat,' etc.; and as it is said in Job, 'When I created the morning star, all my angels praised me[42].' Now by nature light has no warmth.

OF THE FIRMAMENT

ON the evening of the second day of the week, God willed to divide the heavens from the earth, that there might be luminaries and stars beneath the heavens to give light to this world, and that the heavens might be a dwelling-place for the righteous and the angels after the resurrection. God said, 'Let there be a firmament which shall divide the waters from the waters[43]'; and straightway the waters were divided into three parts. One part remained upon the earth for the use of men, cattle, winged fowl--the rivers and the seas; of another part God made the firmament; and the third part He took up above the firmament. But on the day of resurrection the waters will return to their former nature.

OF THE CREATION OF TREES AND PLANTS, AND THE MAKING OF SEAS AND RIVERS

ON the third day God commanded that the waters should be gathered together into the pits and depths of the earth, and that the dry land should appear[44]. When the waters were gathered together into the depths of the earth, and the mountains and hills had appeared, God placed the sand as a limit for the waters of the seas[45], that they might not pass over and cover the earth. And God commanded the earth to put forth herbage and grass and every green thing[46]; and the earth brought forth trees and herbs and plants of all kinds, complete and perfect in respect of flowers and fruit and seed, each according to its kind. Some say that before the transgression of the command, the earth brought forth neither thorns nor briars, and that even the rose had no thorns as it has now; but that after the transgression of the command, the earth put forth thorns and briars by reason of the curse which it had received. The reason why God created the trees and plants before the creation of the luminaries was that the philosophers, who discourse on natural phenomena, might not imagine that the earth brought forth herbs and trees through the power of the heat of the sun. Concerning the making of Paradise, it is not mentioned in the Pentateuch on what day it was created; but according to the opinion of those who may be relied upon, it was made on the same day in which the trees were made[47]: and if the Lord will, we will speak about it in its proper place.

OF THE MAKING OF THE LUMINARIES[48]

ON the fourth day God made the luminaries--sun, moon, and stars--of three substances, air, light, and fire. He took aerial material and prepared vessels like lamps, and mixed fire with light, and filled them. And because in the nature of fire there was no light, nor heat in that of light, the fire imparted heat to the light, and the light gave luminosity to the fire; and from these two were the luminaries--sun, moon, and stars--fabricated. Some say that the luminaries were made in the morning, that the sun was placed in the east, and the moon in the west; while others say that they were made in the evening, and that the sun was placed in the west, and the moon in the east; and therefore the Jews celebrate the fourteenth[49] in the evening. Others say that all the luminaries when they were created were placed in the east; the sun completed his course by day, while the moon waited until eventide, and then began her course. The path of the luminaries is beneath the firmament, and they are not fixed as men have foolishly stated, but the angels guide them. Mâr Isaac says, 'The sun performs his course from the east to the west, and goes behind the lofty northern mountains the whole night until he rises in the east.' And the philosophers say that during the night the luminaries perform their course under the earth.

OF THE CREATION OF SEA-MONSTERS, FISH, WINGED FOWL, AND THE REPTILES THAT ARE IN THE SEAS

ON the fifth day of the week God made from the waters mighty sea-monsters[50], fish, winged fowl, swimming beasts, and the reptiles that are in the seas. He created the winged fowl that are in the waters from the waters; for, like fish, they lay eggs and swim. Now, fish swim in the waters, and winged fowl in the air; but some of the latter in the waters also. Although they say that swimming creatures were made from the waters, or that the other wild beasts and cattle were made from the earth; still they consist of parts of all the other elements. Those, however, that are of the waters, have the greater part of their composition made of water; while the greater part of those whose origin is earth, consists of earth: but none of them lack the four elements.

OF THE CREATION OF BEASTS AND ANIMALS

ON Friday eve God created them[51], and therefore animals can see at night as well as in the day time. Others say that they were all created in the morning, and that God created Adam after them on the sixth day, which is Friday.

OF THE FORMATION OF ADAM

ON the Friday, after the making of all created things, God said, 'Come, let us make man in our image and in our likeness[52].' The Jews have interpreted the expression 'Come, let us make,' as referring to the angels; though God (adored be His glory!) needs not help from His creatures: but the expositors of the Church indicate the Persons of the adorable Trinity. Some say that when God said 'Come, let us make man in our image and in our likeness,' the angels by the eye of the Spirit saw the right hand (of God) spread out over the whole world, and there were in it parts of all the creatures both spiritual and corporeal. And God took from an these parts[53], and fashioned Adam with His holy hands, and breathed into him the breath of life, and man became a living soul[54]. Others say that God took earth from the four quarters of the world[55], and formed Adam outside paradise; while others say that God fashioned him in the middle of the earth, on the spot where our Lord was crucified, and that there also was Adam's skull laid. After God had formed Adam outside Paradise, He brought him in as a king, and made him king over all the creatures, and commanded him to give a name to each of them. God did not gather together unto Adam all cattle, nor (all) that swim in the sea, nor (all) the birds of the air, that he might give them names[56]; but he received dominion and power over them to make use of them as he pleased, and to give them names, as a master to his slaves. And when God had brought him into Paradise, He commanded him to till it and to guard it. Why did God say 'to till it and to guard it'?--for Paradise needed no guarding, and was adorned with fruit of all kinds, and there was none to injure it--unless it were to exhort him to keep His commandments, and to till it that he might not become a lover of idleness. Because Adam had not seen his own formation, and was not acquainted with the power of his Maker, it was necessary that, when Eve was taken from him in his own likeness, he should perceive his Maker, and should acknowledge that He who made Eve also made him, and that they two were bound to be obedient to Him.

OF THE MAKING OF EVE

GOD said, 'Let us make a helper for Adam[57].' And He threw upon Adam a sleep and stupor, and took one of his ribs from his left side, and put flesh in its place, and of it He formed Eve. He did not make her of earth, that she might not be considered something alien to him in nature; and He did not take her from Adam's fore-parts, that she might not uplift herself against him; nor from his hind-parts, that she might not be accounted despicable; nor from his right side, that she might not have pre-eminence over him; nor from his head, that she might not seek authority over him; nor from his feet, that she might not be trodden down and scorned in the eyes of her husband: but (He took her) from his left side[58], for the side is the place which unites and joins both front and back[59].--Concerning the sleep which God cast upon Adam, He made him to be half asleep and half awake, that he might not feel pain when the rib was taken from him, and look upon the woman as a hateful thing; and yet not without pain, that he might not think that she was not meet for him in matters of nature. When Adam came to himself, he prophesied and said, 'This is bone of my bones, and flesh of my flesh; this shall be called woman[60]': and they were both clothed in light, and saw not each other's nakedness.

OF PARADISE

IN the eastern part of the earth, on the mountain of Eden, beyond the ocean, God planted Paradise, and adorned it with fruit-bearing trees of all kinds, that it might be a dwelling-place for Adam and his progeny, if they should keep His commandments. He made to spring forth from it a great river, which was parted into four heads[61], to water Paradise and the whole earth. The first river is Pîshôn, which compasseth the land of Havîlâ, where there is gold and beryls and fair and precious stones. The second river is Gihôn, that is, the Nile of Egypt. The third river is Deklath (the Tigris), which travels through the land of Assyria and Bêth-Zabdai[62]. The fourth river is Perath (the Euphrates), which flows through the middle of the earth. Some teachers say that Paradise surrounds the whole earth like a wall and a hedge beyond the ocean. Others say that it was placed upon the mount of Eden, higher than every other mountain in the world by fifteen cubits[63]. Others say that it was placed between heaven and earth, below the firmament and above this earth, and that God placed it there as a boundary for Adam between heaven and earth, so that, if he kept His commands, He might lift him up to heaven, but if he transgressed them, He might cast him down to this earth. And as the land of heaven is better and more excellent than the land of Paradise, so was the land of Paradise better and more glorious and more excellent (than our earth); its trees were more beautiful, its flowers more odoriferous, and its atmosphere more pure than ours, through superiority of species and not by nature. God made Paradise large enough to be the dwelling-place of Adam and of his posterity, provided that they kept the divine commandments. Now it is the dwelling-place of the souls of the righteous, and its keepers are Enoch and Elijah; Elijah the unwedded, and Enoch the married man: that the unwedded may not exalt themselves above the married, as if, forsooth, Paradise were suitable for the unwedded only. The souls of sinners are without Paradise, in a deep place called Eden. After the resurrection, the souls of the righteous and the sinners will put on their bodies. The righteous will enter into heaven, which will become the land of the righteous; while the sinners will remain upon earth. The tree of good and evil that was in Paradise did not by nature possess these properties of good and evil like rational beings, but only through the deed which was wrought by its means; like the 'well of contention[64],' and the 'heap of witness[65],' which did not possess these properties naturally, but only through the deeds which were wrought by their means. Adam and Eve were not stripped of the glory with which they were clothed, nor did they die the death of sin, because they desired and ate of the fruit of the fig-tree--for the fruit of the fig-tree was not better than the fruit of any other tree--but because of the transgression of the law, in that they were presumptuous and wished to become gods. On account of this foolish and wicked and blasphemous intention, chastisement and penalty overtook them.--Concerning the tree of life which was planted in the middle of Paradise, some have said that Paradise is the mind, that the tree of good and evil is the knowledge of material things, and that the tree of life is the knowledge of divine things, which were not profitable to the simple understanding of Adam[66]. Others have said that the tree of life is the kingdom of heaven and the joy of the world to come; and others that the tree of life was a tree in very truth, which was set in the middle of Paradise, but no man has ever found out what its fruit or its flowers or its nature was like[67].

OF THE SIN OF ADAM[68]

WHEN God in His goodness had made Adam, He laid down a law for him, and commanded him not to eat of the tree of good and evil, which is the fig-tree. After Eve was created, Adam told her the story of the tree; and Satan heard it, and by his envy it became the occasion and cause of their being made to sin, and being expelled from Paradise, for it was by reason of him that Adam fell from the height of his glory. Some say that Satan heard when God commanded Adam not to eat of that tree. Others say that God commanded Adam in his mind, mentally (and not by sense); others again say, by sense and openly. And Satan saw that the serpent was more subtle than all four-footed beasts[69]; and he played in him, as it were with pipes, in the hearing of Eve, like an instrument, and said to her, 'Ye shall not die, as God hath said to you, but ye shall be gods like God, knowers of good and evil.' Then Eve saw that the appearance of the fig-tree was beautiful, and that its smell was delightful; and she desired to eat of it and to become a goddess. So she stretched out her hand, and plucked, and ate, and gave also to her husband, and he likewise did eat. And they were stripped of the fair glory and glorious light of purity wherewith they were clothed, when they saw not each other's nakedness. And their eyes were opened, and they saw their nakedness; and they took leaves of the fig-tree, and covered their nakedness for shame, and hid themselves beneath thick trees. Then God called Adam and said to him, 'Where art thou, Adam?'--not that He did not know where he was, but in a chiding manner--and Adam said, 'Lord, I heard Thy voice, and I hid myself because I am naked.' God said, 'Whence knowest thou that thou art naked? peradventure hast thou transgressed the law and command which I laid down for thee, and hast eaten of the tree of which I commanded thee not to eat?' Adam said, 'The woman whom thou gavest to be with me, she gave to me, and I did eat.' And God questioned Eve in like manner; and Eve said, 'The serpent beguiled me, and I did eat.' And God cursed the serpent, saying, 'Cursed art thou above all beasts upon the earth.' With the cursing of the serpent, who was the tool of Satan, Satan, who had instigated the serpent, was himself cursed; and immediately his legs were destroyed, and he crawled upon his belly, and instead of being an animal became a hissing reptile. And God set enmity between the serpent and man, saying, 'He shall smite the heel of man, but man shall crush his head, and the food of the serpent shall be dust.' God said to Eve, 'In pain shalt thou bring forth children;' and to Adam He said, 'Cursed is the ground for thy sake, and in toil and the sweat of thy face shalt thou eat thy bread; for dust thou art, and unto dust shalt thou return.' And the earth, by reason of the curse which it had received, straightway brought forth thorns and thistles. And God drove them out from Paradise at the ninth hour of the same day in which they were created.

OF THE EXPULSION OF ADAM AND EVE FROM PARADISE

AFTER God had expelled them from Paradise, like wicked servants driven forth from the inheritance of their master, and had cast them into exile, over the gate at the eastern side of Paradise He set a cherub with a sword and spear to frighten Adam from approaching Paradise. Some say that the cherub was one of the heavenly hosts, of the class of the Cherubim; and others say that he did not belong to the spiritual powers, but was a terrible form endowed with a body. So also the spear point and the sword were made of fire extended like a sharp sword, which went and came round about Paradise to terrify Adam and his wife. And God made for them garments of skin to cover their shame. Some say that they clothed themselves with the skins of animals, which they stripped off; but this is not credible, for all the beasts were created in couples, and Adam and Eve had as yet no knives to kill and flay them; hence it is clear that he means the bark of trees[70]. Only the blessed Moses called the bark of trees 'skins,' because it fills the place of skins to trees. In the land of India there are trees whose bark is used for the clothing of kings and nobles and the wealthy, on account of its beauty. After God had expelled Adam and his wife from Paradise, He withheld from them the fruits of trees, and the use of bread and flesh and wine, and the anointing with oil; but they cooked grain and vegetables and the herbs of the earth, and did eat sparingly. Moreover, the four-footed beasts and fowl and reptiles rebelled against them, and some of them became enemies and adversaries unto them. They remained thus until Noah went forth from the ark, and then God allowed them to eat bread and to drink wine and to eat flesh, after they had slain the animal and poured out its blood. They say that when Adam and Eve were driven out of Paradise, Adam cut off a branch for a staff from the tree of good and evil; and it remained with him, and was handed down from generation to generation unto Moses and even to the Crucifixion of our Lord; and if the Lord will, we will relate its history in its proper place[71].

OF ADAM'S KNOWING EVE

WHEN Adam and Eve went forth from Paradise, they were both virgins. After thirty years Adam knew Eve his wife, and she conceived and brought forth Cain together with his sister Kelêmath at one birth[72]. And after thirty years Eve conceived and brought forth Abel and Lebôdâ his sister at one birth. And when they arrived at the age for marriage, Adam wished and intended to give Abel's sister to Cain and Cain's sister to Abel; but Cain desired his own sister more than Abel's[73]. Both (i.e. Kelêmath and Lebôdâ) were his sisters, but because of their birth at one time I have called them thus. Now Cain's sister was exceedingly beautiful. The two brothers made an offering to God because of this matter. Abel, because he was a shepherd, offered up of the fat firstlings of his flock in great love, with a pure heart and a sincere mind. Cain, because he was a husbandman, made an offering of some of the refuse of the fruits of his husbandry with reluctance. He made an offering of ears of wheat that were smitten by blight; but some say of straw only. And the divine fire came down from heaven and consumed the offering of Abel, and it was accepted; while the offering of Cain was rejected. And Cain was angry with God, and envied his brother; and he persuaded his brother to come out into the plain, and slew him. Some say that he smashed his head with stones, and killed him; and others say that Satan appeared to him in the form of wild beasts that fight with one another and slay each other. At any rate, he killed him, whether this way or that way. Then God said to Cain, 'Where is Abel thy brother?' Cain said, 'Am I forsooth my brother's keeper?' God said, 'Behold, the sound of the cry of thy brother Abel's blood has come unto me;' and God cursed Cain, and made him a wanderer and a fugitive all the days of his life. From the day in which the blood of Abel was shed upon the ground, it did not again receive the blood of any animal until Noah came forth from the ark. Adam and Eve mourned for Abel one hundred years. In the two hundred and thirtieth year[74], Seth, the beautiful, was born in the likeness of Adam; and Adam and Eve were consoled by him, Cain and his descendants went down and dwelt in the plain, while Adam and his children, that is the sons of Seth, dwelt upon the top of the Mount of Eden, And the sons of Seth went down and saw the beauty of the daughters of Cain, and lay with them[75]; and the earth was corrupted and polluted with lasciviousness[76]; and Adam and Eve heard of it and mourned.

Now Adam lived nine hundred and thirty years[77]. Some say that in the days of Seth the knowledge of books went forth in the earth; but the Church does not accept this. When Seth was two hundred and fifty years old[78], he begat Enos; and Seth lived nine hundred and thirteen years[79], and he died. Enos was two hundred and ninety years[80] old when he begat Cainan; and Enos first called upon the name of the Lord. Some say that he first composed books upon the course of the stars and the signs of the Zodiac[81]. Enos lived nine hundred and five years. Cainan was a hundred and forty[82] years old when he begat Mahalaleel; and he lived nine hundred and ten years. Mahalaleel was one hundred and sixty-five[83] years old when he begat Jared; and he lived eight hundred and ninety-five years[84]. Jared was one hundred and sixty-two years old when he begat Enoch; and he lived nine hundred and sixty-two years. Enoch was one hundred and sixty-five[85] years old when he begat Methuselah; and when he was three hundred and sixty-five years old, God removed him to the generation of life, that is to Paradise. Methuselah was one hundred and eighty-seven years old when he begat Lamech; and he lived nine hundred and sixty-nine years. Lamech was a hundred and eighty-two years old when he begat Noah; and he lived seven hundred and seventy-seven years[86].

OF THE INVENTION OF THE INSTRUMENTS FOR WORKING IN IRON[87]

SOME say that Cainan[88] and Tubal-cain, who were of the family of Cain, were the first who invented the three tools of the art of working in iron, the anvil, hammer and tongs. The art of working in iron is the mother and begetter of all arts; as the head is to the body, so is it to all other crafts. And as all the limbs of the body cease to perform their functions if the head is taken away from it, so also all other arts would cease if the art of working in iron were to come to an end. In the days of Tubal and Tubal-cain, the sons of Lamech the blind, Satan entered and dwelt in them, and they constructed all kinds of musical instruments, harps and pipes. Some say that spirits used to go into the reeds and disturb them, and that the sound from them was like the sound of singing and pipes[89]; and men constructed all kinds of musical instruments. Now this blind Lamech was a hunter, and could shoot straight with a bow; his son used to take him by the hand, and guide him to places where there was game, and when he heard the movement of an animal, he shot an arrow at it, and brought it down. One day, when shooting an arrow at an animal, he smote Cain the murderer, the son of Adam, and slew him[90].

OF NOAH AND THE FLOOD[91]

WHEN Noah was five hundred years old, he took a wife from the daughters of Seth; and there were born to him three sons, Shem, Ham and Japhet. And God saw Noah's uprightness and integrity, while all men were corrupted and polluted by lasciviousness[92]; and He determined to remove the human race from this broad earth, and made this known to the blessed Noah, and commanded him to make an ark for the saving of himself, his sons, and the rest of the animals. Noah constructed this ark during the space of one hundred years, and he made it in three stories[93], all with boards and projecting ledges. Each board was a cubit long and a span broad. The length of the ark was three hundred cubits, its width fifty cubits, and its height thirty cubits. Noah made it of box wood, though some say of teak wood; and he pitched it within and without. At the end of the six hundredth year, God commanded Noah, with his wife, his sons and his daughters-in-law--eight souls--to go into the ark[94], and to take in with him seven couples of every clean animal and fowl, and one couple of every unclean animal, a male and a female. And he took bread and water in with him according to his need: not an abundant supply, lest they might be annoyed by the smell of the faeces, but they got food just sufficient to preserve their lives. God forewarned the blessed Noah of what he was about to do seven days beforehand, in case the people might remember their sins and offer the sacrifice of repentance. But those rebels mocked at him scoffingly, and thrust out their unclean lips at the sound of the saw and the adze. After seven days God commanded Noah to shut the door of the ark, and to plaster it over with bitumen[95]. And the fountains of the deeps were broken up from beneath, and a torrent of rain (fell) from above, for forty days and forty nights, without cessation, until the waters rose fifteen cubits above the highest mountains in the world. And the waters bore up the ark, which travelled over them from east to west and from north to south, and so inscribed the figure of the cross upon the world; and it passed over the ocean, and came to this broad earth[96]. So the rain was stayed, and the winds blew, and the waters remained upon the earth without diminishing one hundred and fifty days, besides those forty days; which, from the time that Noah entered the ark and the flood began until the waters began to diminish, make in all one hundred and ninety days, which are six months and ten days--even until the twentieth day of the latter Teshrî. The waters began to diminish from the latter Teshrî to the tenth month, on the first day of which the tops of the mountains appeared, but until the time when the earth was dry, and the dove found rest for the sole of her foot, was one hundred days. The ark rested upon the top of mount Kardô[97]. In the tenth month, which is Shebât[98], Noah opened the door of the ark, and sent a raven to bring him news of the earth. And it went and found dead bodies, and it alighted upon them and returned not. For this reason people have made a proverb about Noah's raven. Again he sent forth a dove, but it found not a place whereon to alight, and returned to the ark. After seven days he sent forth another dove, and it returned to him in the evening carrying an olive leaf in its bill; and Noah knew that the waters had subsided. Noah remained in the ark a full year, and he came forth from it and offered up an offering of clean animals; and God accepted his offering and promised him that He would never again bring a flood upon the face of the earth, nor again destroy beasts and men by a flood; and He gave him (as) a token the bow in the clouds, and from that day the bow has appeared in the clouds; and He commanded him to slay and eat the flesh of beasts and birds after he had poured out their blood. The number of people who came forth from the ark was eight souls, and they built the town of Themânôn[99] after the name of the eight souls, and it is to-day the seat of a bishopric in the province of Sûbâ[100]. Noah planted a vineyard, and drank of its wine; and one day when he slumbered, and was sunk in the deep sleep of drunkenness, his nakedness was uncovered within his tent. When Ham his son saw him, he laughed at him and despised him, and told his brethren Shem and Japhet. But Shem and Japhet took a cloak upon their shoulders, and walked backwards with their faces turned away, and threw the cloak over their father and covered him, and then they looked upon him. When Noah awoke and knew what had been done to him by the two sets of his sons, he cursed Canaan the son of Ham and said, 'Thou shalt be a servant to thy brethren;' but he blessed Shem and Japhet. The reason why he cursed Canaan, who was not as yet born nor had sinned, was because Ham had been saved with him in the ark from the waters of the flood, and had with his father received the divine blessing; and also because the arts of sin--I mean music and dancing and all other hateful things--were about to be revived by his posterity, for the art of music proceeded from the seed of Canaan[101]. After the flood a son was born to Noah, and he called his name Jônatôn[102]; and he provided him with gifts and sent him to the fire of the sun, to the east. Noah lived after the flood three hundred and fifty years;

the sum of his years was nine hundred and fifty years; and he saw eighteen generations and families before and after it. He died on the fourth day of the week, on the second of Nîsân, at the second hour of the day; his son Shem embalmed him, and his sons buried him, and mourned over him forty days.

OF MELCHIZEDEK[103]

NEITHER the father nor mother of this Melchizedek were written down in the genealogies; not that he had no natural parents[104], but that they were not written down. The greater number of the doctors say that he was of the seed of Canaan, whom Noah cursed. In the book of Chronography, however, (the author) affirms and says that he was of the seed of Shem the son of Noah. Shem begat Arphaxar, Arphaxar begat Cainan, and Cainan begat Shâlâh and Mâlâh, Shâlâh was written down in the genealogies; but Mâlâh was not, because his affairs were not sufficiently important to be written down in the genealogies. When Noah died, he commanded Shem concerning the bones of Adam, for they were with them in the ark, and were removed from the land of Eden to this earth. Then Shem entered the ark, and sealed it with his father's seal, and said to his brethren, 'My father commanded me to go and see the sources of the rivers and the seas and the structure of the earth, and to return.' And he said to Mâlâh the father of Melchizedek, and to Yôzâdâk his mother, 'Give me your son that he may be with me, and behold, my wife and my children are with you.' Melchizedek's parents said to him, 'My lord, take thy servant; and may the angel of peace be with thee, and protect thee from wild beasts and desolation of the earth.' Shem went by night into the ark, and took Adam's coffin; and he sealed up the ark, saying to his brethren, 'My father commanded me that no one should go into it.' And he journeyed by night with the angel before him, and Melchizedek with him, until they came and stood upon the spot where our Lord was crucified. When they had laid the coffin down there, the earth was rent in the form of a cross[105], and swallowed up the coffin, and was again sealed up and returned to its former condition. Shem laid his hand upon Melchizedek's head, and blessed him, and delivered to him the priesthood, and commanded him to dwell there until the end of his life. And he said to him, 'Thou shalt not drink wine nor any intoxicating liquor, neither shall a razor pass over thy head; thou shalt not offer up to God an offering of beasts, but only fine flour and olive oil and wine; thou shalt not build a house for thyself; and may the God of thy fathers be with thee.' And Shem returned to his brethren, and Melchizedek's parents said to him, 'Where is our son?' Shem said, 'He died while he was with me on the way, and I buried him;' and they mourned for him a month of days; but Melchizedek dwelt in that place until he died. When he was old, the kings of the earth heard his fame, and eleven of them gathered together and came to see him; and they entreated him to go with them, but he would not be persuaded. And when he did not conform to their wishes, they built a city for him there, and he called it Jerusalem; and the kings said to one another, 'This is the king of all the earth, and the father of nations.' When Abraham came back from the battle of the kings and the nations, he passed by the mount of Jerusalem; and Melchizedek came forth to meet him, and Abraham made obeisance to Melchizedek, and gave him tithes of all that he had with him. And Melchizedek embraced him and blessed him, and gave him bread and wine from that which he was wont to offer up as an offering.

OF THE GENERATIONS OF NOAH[106]

THE children of Shem. The people of Shem are twenty and seven families. Elam, from whom sprang the Elamites; Asshur, from whom sprang the Assyrians (Âthôrâyê); Arphaxar[107], from whom sprang the Persians; and Lud (Lôd) and Aram, from whom sprang the Arameans, the Damascenes, and the Harranites. Now the father of all the children of Eber was Arphaxar. Shâlâh begat Eber (Abâr), and to Eber were born two sons; the name of the one of whom was Peleg (Pâlâg), because in his days the earth was divided. From this it is known that the Syriac language remained with Eber, because, when the languages were confounded and the earth was divided, he was born, and was called Peleg by the Syriac word which existed in his time. After Peleg, Joktân (Yaktân) was born, from whom sprang the thirteen nations who dwelt beside one another and kept the Syriac language. And their dwelling was from Menashshê (or Manshâ) of mount Sepharvaïm[108], by the side of the land of Canaan, and towards the east, beginning at Aram and Damascus, and coming to Baishân [Maishân ?] and Elam, and their border (was) Assyria, and the east, and Persia to the south, and the Great Sea[109]. Now the Hebrew has Maishân instead of Menashshê (or Manshâ), in the verse, 'The children of Joktân dwelt from Maishân to Sepharvaïm[110].'

The children of Ham. The people of Ham are thirty and six families, besides the Philistines and Cappadocians. Cush, from whom sprang the Cushites; Misraim, from whom sprang the Misrâyê (or Egyptians); Phut (or Pôt), from whom sprang the Pôtâyê; Canaan, from whom sprang the Canaanites; the seven kings whom Joshua the son of Nun destroyed[111]; the children of 'Ôbâr[112], Shebâ and Havîlâ, from whom sprang the Indians, the Amorites, the Samrâyê, the Metrâyê, and all the dwellers of the south. And of Cush was born Nimrod, who was the first king after the flood. The beginning of his kingdom was Babel (Babylon), which he built, and in which he reigned; and then, after the division of tongues, he built the following cities: Ârâch (Erech), which is Orhâi (Edessa), Âchâr (Accad), which is Nisîbis, and Calyâ (Calneh), which is Ctesiphon[113]. The land of Babel he called the land of Shinar[114], because in it were the languages confounded[115], for 'Shinar' in the Hebrew language is interpreted 'division.' From that land the Assyrian went forth and built Nineveh and the town of Rehôbôth, which is the town of Arbêl (Irbil). It is said that Belus, the son of Nimrod, was the first to depart from Babel and to come to Assyria; and after Belus, his son Ninus built Nineveh, and called it after his name, and Arbêl and Câlâh, which is Hetrê (Hatrâ)[116], and Resen, which is Rêsh-`ainâ (Râs`ain). Misraim begat Ludim, from whom sprang the Lôdâyê; La`bîm, from whom sprang the Lûbâyê; Lahbîm, from whom sprang the Tebtâyê; Yaphtuhîm, Pathrusîm, and Casluhîm, from whom went forth the Philistines, the Gedrâyê (Gadarenes), and the people of Sodom. Canaan begat Sidon his firstborn, from whom sprang the Sôrâyê (Tyrians) and Sidonians, ten nations who dwelt by the side of Israel, from the sea (i.e. the Mediterranean) to the Euphrates; the Kîshâyê, the Kenrâyê (or Kîrâyê), and the Akdemônâyê (or Kadmônâyê), who were between the children of Esau and Amnâ of Ireth[117]. The children of Lot are children of Ham[118].

The children of Japhet. The people of Japhet are fifteen families. Gomer, from whom sprang the Gêothâyê (Gôthâyê, Goths ?); Magog, from whom sprang the Galatians; Mâdâi, from whom sprang the Medes; Javan, from whom sprang the Yaunâyê (Greeks); Tûbîl (Tubal), from whom sprang the Baithônâyê (Bithynians); Meshech, from whom sprang the Mûsâyê (Mysians); Tîras, from whom sprang the Tharnekâyê (or Thrêkâyê, Thracians), the Anshklâyê (or Asklâyê), and the Achshklâyê. The children of Gomer: Ashkenaz, from whom sprang the Armenians; Danphar, from whom sprang the Cappadocians; Togarmah, from whom sprang the Asâyê (Asians) and the Îsaurâyê (Isaurians). The sons of Javan: Elisha, that is Halles (Hellas); Tarshîsh, Cilicia, Cyprus, Kâthîm (Kittîm), Doranim[119], and the Macedonians; and from these they were divided among the islands of the nations. These are the families of the children of Noah, and from them were the nations divided on the earth after the flood; they are seventy and two families, and according to the families, so are the languages.

OF THE SUCCESSION OF GENERATIONS FROM THE FLOOD UNTIL NOW[120]

SHEM was a hundred years old, and begat Arphaxar two years after the flood; the sum of his years was six hundred. Arphaxar was a hundred and thirty-five years old, and begat Kainan. Kainan was a hundred and thirty-nine years old, and begat Shâlâh: the sum of his years was four hundred and thirty-eight. Shâlâh was a hundred and thirty years old[121], and begat Eber; the sum of his years was four hundred and thirty-three. Eber was a hundred and thirty-four years old, and begat Peleg; the sum of his years was four hundred and sixty-four. Peleg was a hundred and thirty years old, and begat Reu; the sum of his years was a hundred and thirty-nine. In the days of Reu the languages were divided into seventy and two; up to this time there was only one language[122], which was the parent of them all, namely, Aramean, that is Syriac. Reu was a hundred and thirty-two years old, and begat Serug; the sum of his years was a hundred and thirty-nine[123]. Serug was a hundred and thirty years old, and begat Nahor; the sum of his years was a hundred and thirty years[124]. In the days of Serug men worshipped idols and graven images. Nahor was seventy and nine years old[125], and begat Terah; the sum of his years was one hundred and forty-eight. In the days of Nahor magic began in the world[126]. And God opened the storehouse of the winds and whirlwinds[127], and they uprooted the idols and graven images, and they collected them together and buried them under the earth, and they reared over them these mounds that are in the world. This was called 'the Wind Flood.' Terah was seventy years old, and begat Abraham; the sum of his years was one hundred and five years[128]. So it is two thousand two hundred and forty-two years from Adam to the flood; and one thousand and eighty-one years from the flood to the birth of Abraham; and from Adam to Abraham it is three thousand three hundred and thirteen years[129]. And know, my brother readers, that there is a great difference between the computation of Ptolemy[130] and that of the Hebrews and the Samaritans; for the Jews take away one hundred years from the beginning of the years of each (patriarch), and they add them to the end of the years of each of them, that they may disturb the reckoning and lead men astray and falsify the coming of Christ, and may say, 'The Messiah is to come at the end of the world, and in the last times;' and behold, according to their account, He came in the fourth millenium, for so it comes out by their reckoning.

OF THE BUILDING OF THE TOWER AND THE DIVISION OF TONGUES[131]

WHEN Reu was born in the days of Peleg, the sons of Noah, Shem, Ham, and Japhet, together with Arphaxar and their children, were gathered together in Shinar. And they took counsel together, saying, 'Come, let us build for ourselves a high tower, the top of which shall be in the heavens, lest a flood come again upon us, and destroy us from off the face of the earth.' And they began to make bricks and to build, until (the tower) was reared a great height from the ground. Then they determined to build seventy-two other towers around it, and to set up a chief over each tower to govern those who were under his authority. God saw the weariness of their oppression and the hardness of their toil, and in His mercy had compassion upon them; for the higher they went, the more severe became their labour, and their pain went on increasing, by reason of the violence of the winds and storms and the heat of the luminaries and the necessity of carrying up everything they needed. And God said, 'Come, let us go down and divide the tongues there.' The expression 'Come, let us,' resembles 'Come, let us make man in our image and in our likeness,' and refers to the persons of the adorable Trinity. While they were tormenting themselves with that vain labour, their language was suddenly confounded so as to become seventy-two languages, and they understood not each other's speech, and were scattered throughout the whole world, and built cities, every man with his fellow who spoke the same language. From Adam to the building of the tower, there was only one language, and that was Syriac. Some have said that it was Hebrew; but the Hebrews were not called by this name until after Abraham had crossed the river Euphrates and dwelt in Harrân; and from his crossing they were called Hebrews. It was grievous to Peleg that the tongues were confounded (or, that God had confounded the tongues of mankind) in his days, and he died; and his sons Serug and Nahor buried him in the town of Pâlgîn, which he built after his name.

OF ABRAHAM[132]

TERAH the father of Abraham took two wives; the one called Yônâ, by whom he begat Abraham; the other called Shelmath, by whom he begat Sarah. Mâr Theodore says that Sarah was the daughter of Abraham's uncle, and puts the uncle in the place of the father. When Abraham was seventy-five years old, God commanded him to cross the river Euphrates and to dwell in Harrân. And he took Sarah his wife and Lot his nephew, and crossed the river Euphrates and dwelt in Harrân. In his eighty-sixth year his son Ishmael was born to him of Hagar the Egyptian woman, the handmaid of Sarah, whom Pharaoh the king gave to her when he restored her to Abraham; and God was revealed to him under the oak of Mamre. Abraham was a hundred years old when Isaac, the son of promise, was born to him; and on the eighth day he circumcised himself, his son, and every one born in his house. When God commanded Abraham to offer up Isaac upon the altar, He sent him for sacrifice to the special place where, according to the tradition of those worthy of belief, our Lord was crucified. After the death of Sarah, Abraham took to wife Kentôrah (Keturah), the daughter of Yaktân, the king of the Turks. When Isaac was forty years old, Eliezer the Damascene, the servant of Abraham, went down to the town of Arâch (Erech), and betrothed Raphkâ (Rebecca), the daughter of Bethuel the Aramean, to Isaac his lord's son. And Abraham died at the age of one hundred and seventy-five years, and was laid by the side of Sarah his wife in the 'double cave[133,]' which he bought from Ephron the Hittite; When Isaac was sixty years old, there were born unto him twin sons, Jacob and Esau: At that time Arbêl was built; some say that the king who built it was called Arbôl. In Isaac's sixty-sixth year Jericho was built. Esau begat Reuel; Reuel begat Zerah; Zerah begat Jobab, that is Job.

OF THE TEMPTATION OF JOB[134]

THERE was a man in the land of Uz whose name was Job. And he was a perfect, righteous and God-fearing man; and there were born unto him seven sons and three daughters. The number of his possessions was seven thousand sheep, three thousand camels, five hundred yoke of oxen, five hundred she-asses, and a very large train of servants. This man was the greatest of all the children of the east. His children used to go and make a feast; and the day came that his sons and his daughters were eating and drinking in the house of their eldest brother. There came a messenger to Job and said to him, 'The oxen were drawing the ploughs, and the she-asses were feeding by their side, when robbers fell upon them and carried them off, and the young men were slain by the sword; and I alone have escaped to tell thee.' While he was yet speaking, there came another and said to him, 'The fire of God fell from heaven and consumed the sheep and the shepherds, and burnt them up; and I alone have escaped to tell thee.' While he was yet speaking, there came another and said to him, 'The Chaldeans divided themselves into three bands and fell upon the camels and carried them off, and slew the young men; and I alone have escaped to tell thee.' While he was yet speaking, there came another and said to him, 'Thy sons and thy daughters were eating and drinking in the house of their eldest brother, when there came a mighty wind and beat upon the corners of the house, and it fell upon the young people and they are dead; and I alone have escaped to tell thee.' Then Job stood up and rent his garment, and shaved his head; and he fell upon the ground and prostrated himself, saying, 'Naked came I out of my mother's womb, and naked shall I return: the Lord gave, and the Lord hath taken away; blessed be the name of the Lord.' In all this did Job sin not, neither did he blaspheme God. And Satan smote Job with a grievous sore from the sole of his foot to his head (lit. brain); and Job took a potsherd to scrape himself with, and sat upon ashes. His wife says to him, 'Dost thou still hold fast by thy integrity? curse God and die.' Job says to her, 'Thou speakest as one of the foolish women speaketh: we have received the good things of God; shall we not receive His evil things?' In all this did Job sin not, neither did he blaspheme God with his lips. Job's three friends heard of this evil which had come upon him, and they came to him, every man from his own land, to comfort him; and their names were these: Eliphaz the Temanite, Bildad the Shuhite, and

Zophar the Naamathite. When they were come, they lifted up their eyes from afar off, and they did not know him. And they lifted up their voice and wept, and each man rent his garment, and they strewed dust upon their heads towards heaven; and they sat with him upon the ground seven days and seven nights, and none spake a word, for they saw that his blow was very sore. And when he held fast by his God, He blessed him, and gave him seven sons and three daughters; and there were not found in the whole land women more beautiful than Job's daughters, and their names were Jemima, Keren-happuch, and Kezia. And God gave him fourteen thousand sheep, six thousand camels and a thousand yoke of oxen; and Job lived one hundred and forty years after his temptation, and died in peace.

OF THE BLESSINGS OF ISAAC[135]

JACOB was seventy-seven years old when his father Isaac blessed him; and he stole the blessings and birthright from his brother Esau, and fled from before his brother to Harrân. On the first night Jacob saw a ladder reaching from earth to heaven, with angels ascending and descending, and the Power of God upon the top thereof. And he woke and said, 'This is the house of the Lord.' He took the stone that was under his head, and set it up for an altar; and he vowed a vow to God. Now the ladder was a type of Christ's crucifixion; the angels that were ascending and descending were a type of the angels who announced the glad tidings to the shepherds on the day of our Saviour's birth. The Power of God which was upon the top of the ladder was (a type of) the manifestation of God the Word in pure flesh of the formation of Adam. The place in which the vision appeared was a type of the church; the stone under his head, which he set up for an altar, was a type of the altar; and the oil which he poured out upon it was like the holy oil wherewith they anoint the altar.

And Jacob went to Laban the Aramean, his mother's brother, and served before him as a shepherd for fourteen years. And he took his two daughters to wife; Leah with her handmaid Zilpah, and Rachel with her handmaid Bilhah. Now he loved Rachel more than Leah, because she was the younger and was fair in aspect, while Leah had watery eyes. There were born to Jacob by Leah six sons: Rûbîl (Reuben), which is interpreted 'Great is God' (now Jacob was eighty-four years old at that time); Simeon, which is interpreted 'the Obedient;' Levi, that is 'the Perfect;' Judah, that is 'Praise;' Issachar, that is 'Hope is near;' and Zebulun, that is 'Gift' or 'Dwelling-place.' Two sons were born to him by Rachel: Joseph, that is 'Addition;' and Benjamin, that is 'Consolation.' By Zilpah two sons were born to him: Gad, that is 'Luck;' and Asher, that is 'Praise.' By Bilhah two sons were born to him: Dan, that is 'Judgment;' and Naphtali, that is 'Heartener[136];' and one daughter, whose name was Dinah[137]. After twenty years Jacob returned to Isaac; and Isaac lived one hundred and eighty years[138]. Twenty-three years after Jacob went up to his father, Joseph was sold by his brethren to the Midianites for twenty dînârs[139]. When Isaac died, Jacob was one hundred and twenty years old.

OF JOSEPH[140]

AFTER Jacob's sons had been born to him by Leah, then Joseph and Benjamin were born to him (by Rachel); and he loved Joseph more than all his children, because he was the child of (his) old age, and because of his beauty and purity, and his being left motherless. He made him a garment with long sleeves, and his brethren envied him. And he dreamed dreams twice, and their hatred increased, and they kept anger in their hearts against him. They sold him to the Midianites, who carried him to Egypt, and sold him to Potiphar, the chief of the guards; and Potiphar delivered his house and servants into his hands; but because of the wantonness of Potiphar's wife, he was bound and kept in prison for two years. When the chief cup-bearer and the chief baker dreamed dreams in one night, and Joseph interpreted them, his words actually came to pass. After Joseph had remained in bondage two years, Pharaoh the king of Egypt saw two dreams in one night; and he was troubled and disturbed, and the sorcerers and enchanters and wise men were unable to interpret his dreams. Then one of those who had been imprisoned with Joseph remembered (him), and they told Pharaoh; and Joseph interpreted his dreams, and Pharaoh made him king over Egypt. And Joseph gathered together and collected the corn of the seven prosperous years, and saved it for the seven years of famine. When the household of Jacob lacked bread, Jacob sent his sons to Egypt to buy corn, and they met Joseph, and he recognised them, but they did not know him. After he had tortured them twice by his harsh words, he at last revealed himself to them, and shewed himself to his brethren. And he sent and brought his father Jacob and all his family--seventy-five souls in number, and they came down and dwelt in the land of Egypt two hundred and thirty years. Concerning that which God spake to Abraham, 'Thy seed shall be a sojourner in a strange land four hundred and thirty years[141];' they were under subjection in their thoughts from the time that God spake to Abraham until they went forth from Egypt. Jacob died in Egypt, and he commanded that he should be buried with his fathers; and they carried him and buried him by the side of his fathers in the land of Palestine. After Joseph died, another king arose, who knew not Joseph, and he oppressed the children of Israel with heavy labour in clay; at that time Moses was born in Egypt. Since many have written the history of the blessed Joseph at great length, and the blessed Mâr Ephraim has written his history in twelve discourses, concerning everything which happened to him from his childhood to his death, as well as another discourse upon the carrying up of his bones (to Palestine), we refrain from writing a long account of him, that we may not depart from the plan which we laid down in making this collection.

OF MOSES AND THE CHILDREN OF ISRAEL[142]

AFTER Joseph was dead, and another king had arisen who knew not the Israelitish people, the people increased and became strong in Egypt. And Pharaoh was afraid of them, and laid a burden upon them, and oppressed them with hard work in clay, and demanded a tale of bricks from them without giving them straw. At that time Moses the son of Amram, the son of Kohath, the son of Levi, was born. Levi was forty-six years old when he begat Kohath; Kohath was sixty-three years old when he begat Amram; and Amram was seventy years old when he begat Moses. When Moses was born, Pharaoh the king commanded to throw the new-born children of the Israelites into the river. Moses was beautiful in appearance, and he was called Pantîl and Amlâkyâ; and the Egyptians used to call him the Shakwîthâ[143] of the daughter of Pharaoh. The name of Moses' mother was Yokâbar (Jochebed). When the command of the king went forth for the drowning of the infants, she made a little ark covered with pitch, and laid the child in it; and she carried it and placed it in a shallow part of the waters of the river Nile (that is Gîhôn); and she sat down opposite (that is, at a distance), to see what would be the end of the child. And Shîpôr[144], the daughter of Pharaoh, came to bathe in the river-- some say that she was called Tharmesîs[145]--and she saw the ark and commanded it to be fetched. When she opened it, and saw that the appearance of the child was beautiful and his complexion comely, she said, 'Verily this child is one of the Hebrews' children;' and she took him, and reared him up as her son. She sought a Hebrew nurse, and the mother of the child Moses came, and became a nurse to him; and he was reared in the house of Pharaoh until he was forty years old. One day he saw Pethkôm[146] the Egyptian, one of the servants of Pharaoh, quarrelling with an Israelite and reviling him. Moses looked this way and that way, and saw no man; and zeal entered into him, and he slew the Egyptian and buried him in the sand. Two days after, he saw two Hebrews quarrelling with one another. And he said to them, 'Ye are brethren; why quarrel ye with one another?' And one of them thrust him away from him, saying, 'Dost thou peradventure seek to kill me as thou didst the Egyptian yesterday?' Then Moses feared lest Pharaoh should perceive (this) and slay him; and he fled to Midian, and sat by the well there. Now Reuel the Midianite had seven daughters, who used to come to that well and water their father's flocks; and the shepherds came and drove them away; and Moses arose and delivered them, and watered their flocks. When they went to their father, he said to them, 'Ye have come quickly to-day.' They said to him, 'An Egyptian rescued us from the hands of the shepherds, and watered the flocks also.' He said to them, 'Why did ye not bring him? Go quickly and call him hither to eat bread with us.' When Moses came to the house of Reuel and dwelt with him, Reuel loved him and gave him his daughter Zipporah the Cushite to wife. And he said to him, 'Go into the house, and take a shepherd's crook, and go feed thy flocks.' When Moses went into the house to take the rod, it drew near to him by divine agency; and he took it and went forth to feed his father-in-law's flocks.

THE HISTORY OF MOSES' ROD

WHEN Adam and Eve went forth from Paradise, Adam, as if knowing that he was never to return to his place, cut off a branch from the tree of good and evil--which is the fig-tree--and took it with him and went forth; and it served him as a staff all the days of his life. After the death of Adam, his son Seth took it, for there were no weapons as yet at that time. This rod was passed on from hand to hand unto Noah, and from Noah to Shem; and it was handed down from Shem to Abraham as a blessed thing from the Paradise of God. With this rod Abraham broke the images and graven idols which his father made, and therefore God said to him, 'Get thee out of thy father's house,' etc. It was in his hand in every country as far as Egypt, and from Egypt to Palestine. Afterwards Isaac took it, and (it was handed down) from Isaac to Jacob; with it he fed the flocks of Laban the Aramean in Paddan Aram. After Jacob Judah his fourth son took it; and this is the rod which Judah gave to Tamar his daughter-in-law, with his signet ring and his napkin, as the hire for what he had done. From him (it came) to Pharez. At that time there were wars everywhere, and an angel took the rod, and laid it in the Cave of Treasures in the mount of Moab, until Midian was built. There was in Midian a man, upright and righteous before God, whose name was Yathrô (Jethro). When he was feeding his flock on the mountain, he found the cave and took the rod by divine agency; and with it he fed his sheep until his old age. When he gave his daughter to Moses, he said to him, 'Go in, my son, take the rod, and go forth to thy flock.' When Moses had set his foot upon the threshold of the door, an angel moved the rod, and it came out of its own free will towards Moses. And Moses took the rod, and it was with him until God spake with him on mount Sinai. When God said to him, 'Cast the rod upon the ground,' he did so, and it became a great serpent; and the Lord said, 'Take it,' and he did so, and it became a rod as at first. This is the rod which God gave him for a help and a deliverance; that it might be a wonder, and that with it he might deliver Israel from the oppression of the Egyptians. By the will of the living God this rod became a serpent in Egypt. By it God spake to Moses; and it swallowed up the rod of Pôsdî the sorceress of the Egyptians. With it Moses smote the sea of Sôph in its length and breadth, and the depths congealed in the heart of the sea. It was in Moses' hands in the wilderness of Ashîmôn, and with it he smote the stony rock, and the waters flowed forth. Then God gave serpents power over the children of Israel to destroy them, because they had angered Him at the waters of strife. And Moses prayed before the Lord, and God said to him, 'Make thee a brazen serpent, and lift it up with the rod, and let the children of Israel look upon it and be healed.' Moses did as the Lord had commanded him, and he placed the brazen serpent in the sight of all the children of Israel in the wilderness; and they looked upon it and were healed. After all the children of Israel were dead, save Joshua the son of Nun and Caleb the son of Yôphannâ (Jephunneh), they went into the promised land, and took the rod with them, on account of the wars with the Philistines and Amalekites. And Phineas hid the rod in the desert, in the dust at the gate of Jerusalem, where it remained until our Lord Christ was born. And He, by the will of His divinity, shewed the rod to Joseph the husband of Mary, and it was in his hand when he fled to Egypt with our Lord and Mary, until he returned to Nazareth. From Joseph his son Jacob, who was surnamed the brother of our Lord, took it; and from Jacob Judas Iscariot, who was a thief, stole it. When the Jews crucified our Lord, they lacked wood for the arms of our Lord; and Judas in his wickedness gave them the rod, which became a judgment and a fall unto them, but an uprising unto many. [147]There were born to Moses two sons; the one called Gershom, which is interpreted 'sojourner;' and the other Eliezer, which is interpreted 'God hath helped me.' Fifty-two years after the birth of Moses, Joshua the son of Nun was born in Egypt[148]. When Moses was eighty years old, God spake with him upon mount Sinai. And the cry of the children of Israel went up to God by reason of the severity of the oppression of the Egyptians; and God heard their groaning, and remembered His covenants with the fathers, Abraham, Isaac and Jacob, to whom He promised that in their seed should all nations be blessed. One day when Moses was feeding the flock of Jethro his father-in-law, the priest of Midian, he and the sheep went from the wilderness to mount Horeb, the mount of God; and the angel of the Lord appeared to him in a flame of fire in a bush, but the bush was not burnt. Moses said, 'I will turn aside and see this wonderful thing, how it is that the fire blazes in the bush, but the bush is not burnt.' God saw that he turned aside to look, and He called to him from within the bush, and said, 'Moses, Moses.' Moses said, 'Here am I, Lord.' God said to him, 'Approach not hither, for the place upon which thou standest is holy.' And God said to him, 'I am the God of Abraham, the God of Isaac, the God of Jacob;' and Moses covered his face, for he was afraid to look at Him. Some say that when God spake with Moses, Moses stammered through fear. And the Lord said to him, 'I have seen the oppression of My people in Egypt, and have heard the voice of their cry, and I am come down to deliver them from the Egyptians, and to carry them up from that land to the land flowing with milk and honey; come, I will send thee to Egypt.' Moses said, 'Who am I, Lord, that I should go to Pharaoh, and bring out those of the house of Israel from Egypt?' God said to him, 'I will be with thee.' Moses said to the Lord, 'If they shall say unto me, What is the Lord's name? what shall I say unto them?' God said, 'אֶהְיֶה אֲשֶׁר אֶהְיֶה, {Hebrew: AeHøYeH AaSheR AeHøYeH} that is, the Being who is the God of your fathers hath sent me to you. This is My name for ever, and this is My memorial to all generations.' God said to Moses, 'Go, tell Pharaoh everything I say to thee.' Moses said to the Lord, 'My tongue is heavy and stammers; how will Pharaoh accept my word?' God said to Moses, 'Behold, I have made thee a god to Pharaoh, and thy brother Aaron a phophet before thee; speak thou with Aaron, and Aaron shall speak with Pharaoh, and he shall send away the children of Israel that they may serve Me. And I will harden the heart of Pharaoh, and I will work My wonders in the land of Egypt, and will bring up My people the children of Israel from thence, and the Egyptians shall know that I am God.' And Moses and Aaron did everything that God had commanded them. Moses was eighty-three years old when God sent him to Egypt. And God said to him, 'If Pharaoh shall seek a sign from thee, cast thy rod upon the ground, and it shall become a serpent.' Moses and Aaron came to Pharaoh, and threw down Moses' rod, and it became a serpent. The sorcerers of Egypt did the same[149], but Moses' rod swallowed up those of the sorcerers; and the heart of Pharaoh was hardened, and he did not send away the people. And God wrought ten signs by the hands of Moses: first, turning the waters into blood; second, bringing up frogs upon them; third, domination of the gnats; fourth, noisome creatures of all kinds; fifth, the pestilence among the cattle; sixth, the plague of boils; seventh, the coming of hail-stones; eighth, the creation of locusts; ninth, the descent of darkness; tenth, the death of the firstborn. When God wished to slay the first-born of Egypt, He said to Moses, 'This day shall be to you the first of months, that is to say, Nisan and the new year. On the tenth of this month, let every man take a lamb for his house, and a lamb for the house of his father; and if they be too few in number (for a whole lamb), let him and his neighbour who is near him share it. Let the lamb be kept until the fourteenth day of this month, and let all the children of Israel slay it at sunset, and let them sprinkle its blood upon the thresholds of their houses with the sign of the cross. This blood shall be to you a sign of deliverance, and I will see (it) and rejoice in you, and Death the destroyer shall no more have dominion over you;' and

Moses and Aaron told the children of Israel all these things. And the Lord commanded them not to go out from their houses until morning; 'for the Lord will pass over the Egyptians to smite their firstborn, and will see the blood upon the thresholds, and will not allow the destroyer to enter their houses.' When it was midnight, the Lord slew the firstborn of the Egyptians, from the firstborn of Pharaoh sitting upon his throne down to the last. And Pharaoh sent to Moses and Aaron, saying, 'Depart from among my people, and go, serve the Lord, as ye have said; and take your goods and chattels with you.' The Egyptians also urged the children of Israel to go forth from among them, through fear of death; and the children of Israel asked chains of gold and silver and costly clothing of the Egyptians, and spoiled them; and the Lord gave them favour in the sight of the Egyptians. The children of Israel set out from Raamses to Succoth, six hundred thousand men; and when they entered Egypt in the days of Joseph, they were seventy-five souls in number. They remained in bodily and spiritual subjection four hundred and thirty years; from the day that God said to Abraham, 'Thy seed shall be a sojourner in the land of Egypt,' from that hour they were oppressed in their minds. When the people had gone out of Egypt on the condition that they should return, and did not return, Pharaoh pursued after them to bring them back to his slavery. And they said to Moses, 'Why hast thou brought us out from Egypt? It was better for us to serve the Egyptians as slaves, and not to die here.' Moses said, 'Fear not, but see the deliverance which God will work for you to-day.' And the Lord said to Moses, 'Lift up thy rod and smite the sea, that the children of Israel may pass over as upon dry land.' And Moses smote the sea, and it was divided on this side and on that; and the children of Israel passed through the depth of the sea as upon dry land. When Pharaoh and his hosts came in after them, Moses brought his rod back over the sea, and the waters returned to their place; and all the Egyptians were drowned. And Moses bade the children of Israel to sing praises with the song 'Then sang Moses and the children of Israel' (Exod. xv. 1).

The children of Israel marched through the wilderness three days, and came to the place called Murrath (Marah) from the bitterness of its waters; and the people were unable to drink that water. And they lifted up their voice and murmured against Moses, saying, 'What shall we drink?' Moses prayed before God, and took absinth-wood[150], which is bitter in its nature, and threw it into the water, and it was made sweet. There did the Lord teach them laws and judgments. And they set out from thence, and on the fifteenth of the second month, which is Îyâr, came to a place in which there were twelve wells and seventy palm-trees[151]. Dâd-Îshô` says in his exposition of Paradise[152] that the sorcerers Jannes and Jambres, who once opposed Moses, lived there. There was a well in that place, and over it was a bucket and brass chain; and devils dwelt there, because that place resembled Paradise. The blessed Mâkarîs (Macarius) visited that spot, but was unable to live there because of the wickedness of those demons; but that they might not boast over the human race, as if forsooth no one was able to live there, God commanded two anchorites, whose names no man knoweth, and they dwelt there until they died. When the children of Israel saw that wilderness, they murmured against Moses, saying, 'It were better for us to have died in Egypt, being satisfied with bread, than to come forth into this arid desert for this people to perish by hunger.' And God said to Moses, 'Behold, I will bring manna down from heaven for you; a cloud shall shade you by day from the heat of the sun, and a pillar of fire shall give light before you by night.' God said to Moses, 'Go up into this mountain, thou, and Aaron thy brother, and Nadab, and seventy chosen elders of the children of Israel, and let them worship from afar; and let Moses come near to Me by himself.' And they did as the Lord commanded them, and Moses drew near by himself, and the rest of the elders remained below at the foot of the mountain; and God gave him commandments. And Moses made known to the people the words of the Lord; and all the people answered with one voice and said, 'Everything that the Lord commands us we will do.' Moses took blood with a hyssop, and sprinkled it upon the people, saying to them, 'This is the blood of the covenant,' and so forth. And God said to Moses, 'Say unto the children of Israel that they set apart for Me gold and silver and brass and purple,' and the rest of the things which are mentioned in the Tôrâh, 'and let them make a tabernacle for Me.' God also shewed the construction thereof to Moses, saying, 'Let Aaron and his sons be priests to Me, and let them serve My altar and sanctuary.' God wrote ten commandments[153] on two tables of stone, and these are they. Thou shalt not make to thyself an image or a likeness; thou shalt not falsify thy oaths; keep the day of the Sabbath; honour thy father and thy mother; thou shalt not do murder; thou shalt not commit adultery; thou shalt not steal; thou shalt not bear false witness; thou shalt not covet thy neighbour's or brother's house; thou shalt not covet the wife of thy kinsman or neighbour, nor his servants, nor his handmaidens. When the children of Israel saw that Moses tarried on the mountain, they gathered together to Aaron and said to him, 'Arise, make us a god to go before us, for we know not what has become of thy brother Moses.' Aaron said to them, 'Bring me the earrings that are in the ears of your wives and children.' When they had brought them to him, he cast a calf from them, and said to the people, 'This is thy god, O Israel, who brought thee out of Egypt;' and they built an altar, and the children of Israel offered up sacrifice upon it. God said to Moses, 'Get thee down to the people, for they have become corrupt.' And Moses returned to the people, and in his hands were the two tablets of stone, upon which the ten commandments were written by the finger of God. When Moses saw that the people had erred, he was angry and smote the tablets upon the side of the mountain and brake them. And Moses brought the calf, and filed it with a file, and threw it into the fire, and cast its ashes into water; and he commanded the children of Israel to drink of that water. And Moses reproached Aaron for his deeds, but Aaron said, 'Thou knowest that the people is stiffnecked.' Then Moses said to the children of Levi, 'The Lord commands you that each man should slay his brother and his neighbour of those who have wrought iniquity;' and there were slain on that day three thousand men. And Moses went up to the mountain a second time, and there were with him two tables of stone instead of those which he brake. He remained on the mountain and fasted another forty days, praying and supplicating God to pardon the iniquity of the people. When he came down from the mountain with the other two tablets upon which the commandments were written, the skin of his face shone, and the children of Israel were unable to look upon his countenance by reason of the radiance and light with which it was suffused; and they were afraid of him. When he came to the people, he covered his face with a napkin; and when he spake with God, he uncovered his face. And Moses said to Hur, the son of his father-in-law Reuel the Midianite, 'We will go to the land which God promised to give us; come with us, and we will do thee good;' but he would not, and returned to Midian. So the children of Israel went along the road to prepare a dwelling-place for themselves; and they lifted up their voice with a cry; and God heard and was angry, and fire went round about them and burnt up the parts round about their camps. They said to Moses, 'Our soul languishes in this wilderness, and we remember the meats of Egypt; the fishes and the cucumbers and the melons and the onions and the leeks and the garlic; and now we have nought save this manna which is before us.' Now the appearance of manna was like that of coriander seed, and they ground it, and made flat cakes of it; and its taste was like bread with oil in it. And the Lord heard the voice of the people weeping each one at the door of his tent, and it was grievous to Him. Moses prayed before the Lord and said, 'Why have I not found favour before Thee? and why hast Thou cast the weight of this people upon me? Did I beget them? Either slay me or let me find favour in Thy sight.' God said to Moses, 'Choose from the elders of the children of Israel seventy men, and gather them together to the tabernacle, and I will come down and speak with thee. And I will take of the spirit and power which is with thee and will lay it upon them, and they shall bear the burden of the people with thee, and thou shalt not bear it by thyself alone;' and Moses told them. Moses gathered together seventy elders from the children of Israel, and the Lord came down in a cloud, and spake with them; and he took of the spirit and power which was with Moses and laid it upon them, and they prophesied. But two elders of the seventy whose names were written down remained in the camp and did not come; the name of the one was Eldad, and that of the other Medad; and they also prophesied in the tabernacle. A young man came and told Moses, and Joshua the son of Nun, the disciple of Moses, said to him, 'My lord, restrain them.' Moses said, 'Be not jealous; would that all the children of Israel were prophets; for the Spirit of God hath come upon them.'

And Moses said to the children of Israel, 'Because ye have wept and have asked for flesh, behold the Lord will give you flesh to eat; not one day, nor two, nor five, nor ten, but a month of days shall ye eat, until it goeth out of your nostrils, and becometh nauseous to you[154].' Moses said (to the Lord), 'This people among whom I am is six hundred thousand men, and hast Thou promised to feed them with flesh for a month of days? If we slay sheep and oxen, it would not suffice for them; and if we collect for them (all) the fish that are in the sea, they would not satisfy them.' And the Lord said to Moses, 'The hand of the Lord shall bring (this) to pass, and behold, thou shalt see whether this happens or not.' By the command of God a wind blew and brought out quails from the sea, and they were gathered around the camp of the children of Israel about a day's journey on all sides; and they were piled upon one another to the depth of two cubits. Each of the children of Israel gathered about ten cors; and they spread them out before the doors of their tents. And the Lord was angry with them, and smote them with death, and many died; and that place was called 'the graves of lust.'

They departed from thence to the place called Haserôth. And Aaron and Miriam lifted up themselves against Moses because of the Cushite woman whom he had married, and they said, 'Has God spoken with Moses only? Behold, He hath spoken with us also.' Now Moses was meeker than all men. And God heard the words of Miriam and Aaron, and came down in a pillar of cloud, and stood at the door of the tabernacle, and called them, and they came forth to Him. The Lord said to them, 'Hear what I will say to you. I have revealed Myself to you in secret, and ye have prophesied in a dream. Not so with My servant Moses, who is trusted in everything, for with him I speak mouth to mouth.' And the Lord was angry with them, and the cloud was taken up from the tabernacle; and Miriam was a leper, and was white as snow. Aaron saw that she was a leper, and said to Moses, 'I entreat thee not to look upon our sins which we have sinned against thee.' Moses made supplication before God, saying, 'Heal her, O Lord, I entreat Thee.' God said to Moses, 'If her father had spat in her face, it would have been right for her to pass the night alone outside the camp for seven days, and then to come in.' So Miriam stayed outside the camp for seven days, and then she was purified.

And God said to Moses, 'Send forth spies, from every tribe a man, and let them go and search out the land of promise.' Moses chose twelve men, among whom were Joshua the son of Nun and Caleb the son of Jephunneh; and they went and searched out the land. And they returned, carrying with them of the fruit of the land grapes and figs and pomegranates. The spies came and said, 'We have not strength to stand against them, for they are mighty men, while we are like miserable locusts in their sight.' And the children of Israel were gathered together to Moses and Aaron, and they lifted up their voice and wept with a great weeping, saying, 'Why did we not die under the hand of the Lord in the wilderness and in Egypt, and not come to this land to die with our wives and children, and to become a laughing-stock and a scorn to the nations?' Joshua the son of Nun and Caleb the son of Jephunneh said to them, 'Fear not; we will go up against them, and the Lord will deliver them into our hands, and we shall inherit the land, as the Lord said to us.' The children of Israel said to one another, 'Come, let us make us a chief and return to Egypt;' and Moses and Aaron fell upon their faces before the people. And Joshua the son of Nun and Caleb the son of Jephunneh rent their clothes and said to the children of Israel, 'The land which we have searched out is a thriving one, flowing with milk and honey, and it is in the power of God to give it to us; do not provoke God.' And the children of Israel gathered together to stone them with stones. And God was revealed in a cloud over the tabernacle openly in the sight of the children of Israel; and He said to Moses, 'How long will these (people) provoke Me? and how long will they not believe in Me for all the wonders which I have wrought among them? Let Me smite them, and I will make thee the chief of a people stronger than they.' Moses said to the Lord, 'O Lord God Almighty, the Egyptians will hear and will say that Thou hast brought out Thy people from among them by Thy power: but when Thou smitest them, they will say, "He slew them in the desert, because He was unable to make them inherit the land which He promised them." And Thou, O Lord, who hast dwelt among this people, and they have seen Thee eye to eye, and Thy light is ever abiding with them, and Thou goest (before them) by night in a pillar of light, and dost shade them with a cloud by day, pardon now in Thy mercy the sins of Thy people, as Thou hast pardoned their sins from Egypt unto here.' God said to Moses, 'Say unto the children of Israel, O wicked nation, I have heard all the words which ye have spoken, and I will do unto you even as ye wish for yourselves. In this desert shall your dead bodies fall, and your families and your children, every one that knows good from evil, from twenty years old and downwards. Their children shall enter the land of promise; but ye shall not enter it, save Caleb the son of Jephunneh and Joshua the son of Nun. Your children shall remain in this wilderness forty years, until your dead bodies decay, according to the number of the days in which ye searched out the land; for each day ye shall be requited with a year because of your sins.' And the spies who had spied out the land with Joshua the son of Nun and Caleb the son of Jephunneh died at once, save Joshua the son of Nun and Caleb the son of Jephunneh. This was very grievous to the people, and the children of Israel said to Moses, 'Behold, we are going up to the land which God promised us.' He said to them, 'God hath turned His face from you; go ye not away from your place.' And they hearkened not to Moses, but went up to the top of the mountain without Moses and the tabernacle; and the Amalekites and Canaanites who dwelt there came out against them and put them to flight. God said to Moses, 'When the children of Israel enter the land of promise, let them offer as offerings fine flour and oil and wine.' Then Korah the son of Zahar (Izhar), and Dathan and Abiram the sons of Eliab, together with their families, and two hundred and fifty men, separated from the children of Israel; and they came to Moses, and made him hear them, and troubled him. And Moses fell upon his face before the Lord and said, 'To-morrow shall every one know whom God chooses. Is that which I have done for you not sufficient for you, that ye serve before the Lord, but ye must seek the priesthood also?' And Moses said unto God, 'O God, receive not their offerings.' And Moses said to them, 'Let every one of you take his censer in his hand, and place fire and incense therein;' and there stood before the Lord on that day two hundred and fifty men holding their censers. The Lord said to Moses, 'Stand aloof from the people, and I will destroy them in a moment.' And Moses and Aaron fell upon their faces, and said to the Lord, 'Wilt Thou destroy all these for the sake of one man who hath sinned?' God said to Moses, 'Tell the children of Israel to go away from around the tents of Korah and his fellows;' and Moses said to the people everything that God had said to him; and the people kept away from the tent of Korah. Then Korah and his family with their wives and children came forth and stood at the doors of their tents. And Moses said to them, 'If God hath sent me, let the earth open her mouth and swallow them up; but if I am come of my own desire, let them die a natural death like every man.' While the word was yet in his mouth, the earth opened, and swallowed them up, and the people that were with them, from man even unto beast; and fear fell upon their companions. The fire went forth from their censers, and burnt up the two hundred and fifty men. Moses said to Eleazar, 'Take their censers and make a casting of them, that they may be a memorial--for they have been sanctified by the fire which fell into them--that no man who is not of the family of Aaron should dare to take a censer in his hand.'

The children of Israel gathered together unto Moses and Aaron and said to them, 'Ye have destroyed the people of the Lord.' And God said to Moses and Aaron in the tabernacle, 'Stand aloof from them, and I will destroy them in a moment.' Moses said to Aaron, 'Take a censer and put fire and incense therein, and go to the people, that God may forgive their sins, for anger has gone forth against them from before the Lord.' And Aaron put incense in a censer, and went to the people in haste, and he saw death destroying the people unsparingly; but with his censer he separated the living from the dead, and the plague was stayed from them. The number of men whom the plague destroyed at that time of the children of Israel was fourteen thousand and seven hundred, besides those who died with the children of Korah; and Aaron returned to Moses. And God said to Moses, 'Let the children of Israel collect from every tribe a rod, and let them write the name of the tribe upon its rod, and the name of Aaron upon (that of) the tribe of Levi, and the rod of the man whom the Lord chooseth shall blossom.' And they did as God had commanded them, and took the rods and placed them in the tabernacle that day. On the morrow Moses went into the tabernacle, and saw the rod of the house of Levi budding and bearing almonds. And Moses brought out all the rods to the children of Israel, and the sons of Levi were set apart for the service of the priesthood before the Lord.

When the children of Israel came to the wilderness of Sîn, Miriam the sister of Moses and Aaron died, and they buried her. And there was no water for them to drink; and the children of Israel murmured against Moses and said,

'Would that we had all died with those who are dead already, and that we had not come hither to die with our beasts and our possessions! Why did the Lord bring us out from Egypt to this desert land, in which there are neither pomegranates nor grapes?' Moses and Aaron went to the tabernacle, and fell upon their faces before the Lord, and the Lord said to them, 'Gather together the children of Israel, and let Moses smite the rock with the rod, and water shall come forth and all the people shall drink;' and Moses called that water 'the water of strife.' The children of Israel gathered themselves together unto Moses and Aaron, and they murmured against them saying, 'Why have ye brought us out to this desert to die of thirst and hunger?' And the Lord was angry with them, and sent serpents upon them, and many of the people died by reason of the serpents. And they gathered themselves together unto Moses and Aaron and said to them, 'We have sinned before God and before you.' God said to Moses, 'Make a serpent of brass, and hang it upon the top of thy rod, and set it up among the people; and let every one whom a serpent shall bite look upon the brazen serpent, and he shall live and not die.' This serpent which Moses set up is a type of the crucifixion of our Lord, as the doctor saith, 'Like the serpent which Moses set up, He set Him up also, that He might heal men of the bites of cruel demons.'

And the children of Israel came to mount Hôr, and Aaron died there; and they wept for him a month of days; and Moses put his garments upon Eleazar his son. The children of Israel began to commit fornication with the daughters of Moab, and to bow down to their idols, and to eat of their sacrifices. The Lord was angry with them, and He commanded Moses to gather together the children of Israel, and to order every man to slay his fellow, and every one who should bow down to Baal Peôr, the idol of the Moabites. When they were all assembled at the door of the tabernacle, Zimri the son of Salô came and took Cosbî the daughter of Zûr, and committed fornication with her in the sight of Moses and all the people; and God smote the people with a pestilence. Then Phinehas the son of Eleazar the priest, the son of Aaron, arose, and thrust them through with a spear, and lifted them up upon the top of it; and the plague was stayed from that hour. This zeal was accounted unto Phinehas as a prayer; as the blessed David says[155], 'Phinehas arose and prayed, and the pestilence was stayed; and it was accounted unto him for merit from generation unto generation, even for ever.' The number of those who died at that time was twenty-four thousand men. God commanded Moses to number the people, and their number amounted to six hundred and one thousand seven hundred and eighty souls. And God commanded Moses to bless Joshua the son of Nun, and to lay his hand upon him, and to set him up before Eleazar the priest and before all the children of Israel; and God gave him wisdom and knowledge and prophecy and courage, and made him ruler of the children of Israel. God commanded the children of Israel to destroy the Midianites. And (Moses) chose from each tribe a thousand men, and they went up against the Midianites and took them captive and spoiled them. And Moses told them to slay every man who had committed fornication with a Midianitish woman, and every Midianitish woman who had committed fornication with a son of Israel, except the virgins whom man had not known. God commanded Moses to set apart one-fiftieth part of the spoil for the sons of Levi, the ministers of the altar and the house of the Lord. The number of the flocks that were gathered together with the children of Israel was six hundred and seventy thousand, and seventy-two thousand oxen, and thirty-two thousand virgins. And the Lord commanded them that when they should pass over the Jordan and come to the land of promise, they should set apart three villages for a place of flight and refuge, that whosoever committed a murder involuntarily might flee thither and dwell in them until the high priest of that time died, when he might return to his family and the house of his fathers. God laid down for them laws and commandments, and these are they. A man shall not clothe himself in a woman's garments, neither shall a woman clothe herself in those of a man[156]. If one sees a bird's nest, he shall drive away the mother, and then take the young ones[157]. A man shall make a fence and an enclosure to his roof, lest any one fall therefrom, and his blood be required of him[158]. Let him that hath a rebellious son, bring him out before the elders, and let them reprimand him; if he turn from his (evil) habit, (goad and well); but if not, let him be stoned[159]. One that is crucified shall not pass the night upon his cross[160]. He that blasphemes God shall be slain[161]. The man that lies with a betrothed woman shall be slain. If she is not betrothed, he shall give her father five hundred dinârs, and take her to wife[162]. And the other commandments.

And Moses gathered together the children of Israel and said to them, 'Behold, I am a hundred and twenty years old, no more strength abideth in me; and God hath said to me, Thou shalt not pass over this river Jordan.' And he called Joshua the son of Nun and said to him in the sight of all the people, 'Be strong and of good courage, for thou shalt bring this people into the land of promise. Fear not the nations that are in it, for God will deliver them into thy hands, and thou shalt inherit their cities and villages, and shalt destroy them[163].'

And Moses wrote down laws and judgements and orders, and gave them into the hands of the priests, the children of Levi. He commanded them that, when they crossed over to the land of promise, they should make a feast of tabernacles and should read aloud these commandments before all the people, men and women; that they might hear and fear the Lord their God[164]. And God said to Moses, 'Behold thou art going the way of thy fathers; call Joshua the son of Nun, thy disciple, and make him stand in the tabernacle, and command him to be diligent for the government of this people; for I know that after thy death they will turn aside from the way of truth, and will worship idols, and I will turn away My face from them[165].' And God said to Moses, 'Get thee up into this mountain of the Amorites which is called Nebo, and see the land of Canaan, and be gathered to thy fathers, even as Aaron thy brother died on mount Hôr.' So Moses died there and was buried, and no man knoweth his grave[166]; for God hid him, that the children of Israel might not go astray and worship him as God. He died at the age of one hundred and twenty years; his sight had not diminished, neither was the complexion of his face changed. And the children of Israel wept for him a month of days in Arbôth Moab.

From Adam then until the death of Moses was three thousand eight hundred and sixty-eight years[167].

When the number of the children of Israel was reckoned up, it amounted to eight hundred thousand, and that of the house of Judah to five hundred thousand. In the Book of Chronicles it is written, 'The children of Israel were a thousand thousand, one hundred thousand and one hundred men; and the house of Judah was four hundred thousand and seven hundred men that drew sword.' Now when they came out of Egypt, they were six hundred thousand[168]; and when they entered Egypt, they were seventy and five souls[169].

OF JOSHUA THE SON OF NUN, AND BRIEF NOTICES OF THE YEARS OF THE JUDGES AND THE KINGS OF THE CHILDREN OF ISRAEL

AFTER Moses was dead, God said to Joshua the son of Nun, 'Moses My servant is dead; now therefore arise, go over this Jordan, thou and all this people, unto the land which I have sworn to their fathers to give them, Every place upon which ye tread shall be yours[170].' So Joshua the son of Nun gathered the people together, and passed over Jordan. Jordan was divided on this side and on that, and the children of Israel passed over as upon dry ground, even as their fathers passed through the sea of Sôph, when they went forth from Egypt[171]. And they took twelve stones from the midst of Jordan, as a memorial for those after them[172]. And they took Jericho, and destroyed it[173]; and Joshua the son of Nun slew thirty-one kings of the foreign nations, and divided the land among them, and he brake their idols and images. These are the names of the kings whom Joshua the son of Nun destroyed[174]. The king of Jericho, the king of Ai, the king of Jerusalem, the king of Hebron, the king of Jarmuth, the king of Lachish, the king of Eglon, the king of Gezer, the king of Debir, the king of Hormah, the king of Geder, the king of Arad[175], the king of Libnah, the king of Adullam[176], the king of Makkedah[177], the king of Bethel, the king of Tappuah, the king of Hepher, the king of Aphek, the king of Lashsharon[178]; the king of Madon, the king of Hazor, the king of Shimron-meron[179], the king of Achshaph, the king of Taanach, the king of Megiddo[180], the king of Rekam (Kadesh), the king of Jokneam[181], the king of Dor and Naphath-Dor, the king of Goiim[182], the king of Tirzah[183],

And as we do not intend to write a complete history of the kings and judges, but only to collect a few matters which may serve for the consolation of the feeble in a time of despondency, behold we pass over them with brief notices. If however any one seeks to know these (things), let him read in the Tôrah and in the Bêth-Mautebhê[184], whence he will understand clearly. Moses ruled the people in the desert forty years[185]. Joshua ruled the people twenty-five years[186]. Judah was ruler of the people forty-eight years[187]. Eglon king of Moab[188] oppressed the people eighteen years. Ahôr (Ehûd) was ruler of the people eighty years[189]. Nâbîn (Jabin) oppressed

Israel twenty years[190]. Deborah and Barak were rulers of the people forty years[191]. The Midianites oppressed Israel seven years[192]. Gideon was ruler of the people forty years[193]. He had seventy sons, who rode with him upon seventy ass colts[194]. Abimelech the son of Gideon was ruler of the people sixty years[195]. Tola the son of Puah was ruler of the people twenty-three years[196]. Jair was ruler of the people twenty-two years[197]. The Philistines and Ammonites oppressed the people eighteen years[198]. Naphthah (Jephthah) was ruler of the people six years[199]. He vowed a vow to the Lord and said, 'Whatsoever cometh forth to meet me from my house, I will offer up as an offering to the Lord.' And his only daughter came forth, and he offered her up as an offering to the Lord. Abîzan (Ibzan) was ruler of the people seven years[200]. He had thirty sons and thirty daughters; he sent out the thirty daughters and brought in thirty daughters-in-law. Elon was a ruler of the people ten years[201]. Acrôn (Abdon) was ruler of the people eight years[202]. The Philistines oppressed Israel forty years[203]. Samson was ruler of the people twenty years[204]. He slew a thousand men with the jawbone of a dead ass. Eli was ruler of the people forty years[205]. From Eli, the ark was in the house of Abinadab twenty years[206]. Samuel was ruler of the people thirty years[207]. Saul was ruler of the people forty[208] years. These years of the Judges (lit. rulers) amount to six hundred and fifty-five[209]. King David reigned forty years[210]. Solomon reigned forty years[211]. Rehoboam reigned seventeen years[212]. Abijah reigned three years[213]. Asa reigned forty-one years[214]. Jehoshaphat reigned twenty-five years[215]. Joram reigned eight years[216]. Ahaziah reigned one year[217]. Athaliah reigned six years[218]. Joash reigned forty years[219]. Amaziah reigned twenty-three years[220]. Uzziah reigned fifty-two years[221]. Jotham reigned sixteen years[222]. Hezekiah reigned twenty-nine years[223]. He prayed before God, and fifteen years were added to his life; and he held back the sun and the moon in their course. Manasseh reigned fifty-five years[224]. He sawed Isaiah with a wooden saw and killed him. Amon reigned two years[225]. Josiah reigned thirty-one years[226]. Jehoahaz reigned three months[227]. Jehoiakim reigned eleven years[228]. Jehoiachin reigned one hundred days[229]. Zedekiah reigned seven years[230]. These years of the kings amount to four hundred and fifty-five years, six months, and ten days[231].

OF THE DEATH OF THE PROPHETS; HOW THEY DIED, AND (WHERE) EACH ONE OF THEM WAS BURIED[232]

MANASSEH the son of Hezekiah slew Isaiah with a wooden saw; he was buried before the outfall of the waters which Hezekiah concealed by the side of Siloah[233].

Hosea the son of Beeri, of the tribe of Issachar, (was) from the town of Be`elmâth. He prophesied mystically about our Lord Jesus Christ who was to come; saying that when He should be born, the oak in Shiloh should be divided into twelve parts; and that He should take twelve disciples of Israel. He died in peace, and was buried in his own land.

Joel the son of Bethuel (Pethuel), of the tribe of Reuben, died in peace in his own land. Others say that Ahaziah the son of Amaziah smote him with a staff upon his head; and while his life was yet in him, they brought him to his own land[234], and after two days he died.

Amos (was) from the land of Tekoa. The priest of Bethel tortured him and afterwards slew him. Others say that it was he whom Ahaziah the son of Amaziah[235] killed with a staff, and he died.

Obadiah from the country of Shechem was the captain of fifty of Ahab's soldiers. He became a disciple of Elijah, and endured many evil things from Ahab, because he forsook him and went after Elijah. However he died in peace. After he followed Elijah, he was deemed worthy of prophecy[236].

Elijah the fiery, of the family of Aaron, (was) from Tashbî[237], a town of the Levites. When this (prophet) was born, his father saw in a dream that one was born, and that they wrapped him in fire instead of swaddling bands, and gave him some of that fire to eat. He came to Jerusalem, and told the priests the vision that he had seen. The learned among the people said to him, 'Fear not, thy son is about to be a fire, and his word shall be like fire, and shall not fall to the ground; he will burn like fire with jealousy of sinners, and his zeal will be accepted before God.' He was taken up in a chariot towards heaven. Some say that his father was called Shôbâkh[238].

Elisha his pupil, from Abêl-Mehôlâh, (was) of the tribe of Reuben. On the day of his birth a great wonder took place in Israel; for the bull[239] which they worshipped in Gilgal lowed, and his voice was heard in Jerusalem. The chief priests in Jerusalem said, 'A mighty prophet is born to-day in Israel at this time, and he will break the images and idols to pieces.' He died in peace, and was buried in Samaria.

Jonah the son of Amittai[240] (was) from Gath-hepher[241], from Kûryath-Âdâmôs[242], which is near to Ascalon and Gaza and the sea coast. After this (prophet) had prophesied to the Ninevites in the time of Sardânâ[243] the king, he did not remain in his own land because the Jews were jealous of him; but he took his mother, and went and dwelt in Assyria. He feared the reproach of the Jews, because he had prophesied, and his prophecy did not come to pass. He also rebuked Ahab the king, and called a famine upon the land and the people. He came to the widow of Elijah, and blessed her, because she received him, and he returned to Judaea. His mother died on the way, and he buried her by the side of Deborah's grave. He lived in the land of Serîdâ, and died two years after the people had returned from Babylon, and was buried in the cave of Kainân[244]. This (prophet) prophesied that when the Messiah should come, the cities of the Jews would be overturned.

Micah the Morashthite (was) of the tribe of Ephraim, and was slain by Joram the son of Ahab. This (prophet) prophesied concerning the destruction of the temple of the Jews, and the abrogation of the Passover on the death of the Messiah. He died in peace, and was buried in Anikâm.

Nahum, from the city of Elkôsh, (was) of the tribe of Simeon. After the death of Jonah this (prophet) prophesied concerning the Ninevites, saying, 'Nineveh shall perish by perpetually advancing waters, and ascending fire;' and this actually took place. He prophesied also concerning the Babylonians, that they would come against the Israelitish people; and therefore they sought to kill him. He prophesied that when the Messiah should be slain, the vail of the temple should be rent in twain[245], and that the Holy Spirit should depart from it. He died in peace, and was buried in his own country.

Habakkuk (was) of the tribe of Simeon, and from the land of Sûar (Zoar)[246]. This (prophet) prophesied concerning the Messiah, that He should come, and abrogate the laws of the Jews. He brought food to Daniel at Babylon by the divine (or, angelic) agency. The Jews stoned him in Jerusalem.

Zephaniah (was) of the tribe of Simeon. He prophesied concerning the Messiah, that He should suffer, and that the sun should become dark, and the moon be hidden. He died in peace in his own land.

Haggai returned from Babylon to Jerusalem when he was young. He prophesied that the people would return, and concerning the Messiah, that He would abrogate the sacrifices of the Jews. He died in peace.

Zechariah the son of Jehoiada returned from Babylon in his old age, and wrought wonders among the people. He died at a great age, and was buried by the side of the grave of Haggai.

Malachi was born after the return of the people, and because of his beauty he was surnamed 'Angel.' He died in peace in his own land.

The Jews stoned Jeremiah the son of Hilkiah in Egypt, because he rebuked them for worshipping idols; and the Egyptians buried him by the side of Pharaoh's palace. The Egyptians loved him much, because he prayed and the beasts died which used to come up from the river Nile and devour men. These beasts were called 'crocodiles.' When Alexander the son of Philip, the Macedonian, came (to Egypt), he made enquiries about his grave, and took and brought him to Alexandria. This (prophet) during his life said to the Egyptians, 'a child shall be born--that is the Messiah--of a virgin, and He shall be laid in a crib[247], and He will shake and cast down the idols.' From that time, and until Christ was born, the Egyptians used to set a virgin and a baby in a crib, and to worship him, because of what Jeremiah said to them, that He should be born in a crib.

Ezekiel the son of Buzi was of the priestly tribe, and from the land of Serîdâ[248]. The chief of the Jews who was in the land of the Chaldeans slew him, because he rebuked him for worshipping idols. He was buried in the grave of Arphaxar, the son of Shem, the son of Noah.

Daniel (was) of the tribe of Judah, and was born in Upper Beth-Horon. He was a man who kept himself from women, and hence the Jews thought that he was an eunuch, for his face was different (from that of other men), and he had no children. He prayed for the Babylonians, and died in Elam, in the city of the Hôzâyê[249], and was buried in Shôshan the fortress. He prophesied concerning the return of the people.

Ahijah (was) from Shilo. A lion slew this prophet, and he was buried by the oak at Shilo in Samaria.

Ezra the scribe was from the country of Sâbthâ[250], and of the tribe of Judah. This (prophet) brought back the people, and died in peace in his own land.

Zechariah the son of Berachiah, the priest, was from Jerusalem. Joash the king slew this (prophet) between the steps[251] and the altar, and sprinkled his blood upon the horns of the altar, and the priests buried him. From that day God forsook the temple, and angels were never again seen in it.

Simon the son of Sîrâ (Sirach) died in peace in his own town.

Nathan died in peace.

Here ends the first part of the book of gleanings called 'the Bee.'

To God be the glory, and may His mercy and compassion be upon us. Amen.

Again, by the Divine power, we write the second part of the book of gleanings called 'the Bee,' regarding the Divine dispensation which was wrought in the new (covenant).

OF THE MESSIANIC GENERATIONS[252]

GOD created Adam. Adam begat Seth. Seth begat Enos. Enos begat Kainân. Kainân begat Mahalaleel. Mahalaleel begat Jared. Jared begat Enoch. Enoch begat Methuselah. Methuselah begat Lamech. Lamech begat Noah. Noah begat Shem. Shem begat Arphaxar. Arphaxar begat Kainân. Kainân begat Shâlâch. Shâlâch begat Eber. Eber begat Peleg. Peleg begat Reu. Reu begat Serug. Serug begat Nahor. Nahor begat Terah. Terah begat Abraham. Abraham begat Isaac. Isaac begat Jacob. Jacob begat Judah. Judah took a Canaanitish wife, whose name was Shuah. And it was very grievous to Jacob, and he said to Judah, 'The God of my fathers will not allow the seed of Canaan to be mingled with our seed, nor his family with our family.' There were born to Judah by the Canaanitish woman three sons, Er, Onan, and Shelah. Er took Tamar, the daughter of Merari the son of Levi, to wife, and he lay with her in the Sodomite way and died without children. After him his brother Onan took her, to raise up seed to his brother; he also, when he lay with her, scattered his seed outside of her on the ground, and he too died without children. Because Shelah was a child, Judah kept his daughter-in-law in widowhood, that he might give her to Shelah to raise up seed by her. But Tamar went into her father-in-law by crafty devices, and lay with him, and conceived, and gave birth to twins, Pharez and Zarah. Pharez begat Hezron. Hezron begat Aram. Aram begat Amminadab. Amminadab begat Nahshon. Eleazar the son of Aaron, the priest, took the sister of Nahshon to wife, and by her begat Phinehas; and the seed of the priesthood was mingled with the royal line[253]. Nahshon begat Salmon. Salmon begat Boaz by Rahab. Boaz begat Obed by Ruth the Moabitess. Obed begat Jesse. Jesse begat David the king by Nahash.

Now two genealogies are handed down from David to Christ; the one from Solomon to Jacob[254], and the other from Nathan to Heli[255]. David begat Solomon. Solomon begat Rehoboam. Rehoboam begat Abijah. Abijah begat Asa. Asa begat Jehoshaphat. Jehoshaphat begat Joram. Joram begat Uzziah. Uzziah begat Jotham. Jotham begat Ahaz. Ahaz begat Hezekiah. Hezekiah begat Manasseh. Manasseh begat Amon. Amon begat Josiah. Josiah begat Jeconiah. Jeconiah begat Salathiel. Salathiel begat Zerubbabel. Zerubbabel begat Abiud. Abiud begat Eliakim. Eliakim begat Azor. Azor begat Zadok. Zadok begat Achin. Achin begat Eliud. Eliud begat Eleazar. Eleazar begat

Matthan. Matthan begat Jacob. Jacob begat Joseph. Or again: David begat Nathan. Nathan begat Mattatha. Mattatha begat Mani. Mani begat Melea. Melea begat Eliakim. Eliakim begat Jonam. Jonam begat Levi[256]. Levi begat Mattîtha. Mattîtha begat Jorim. Jorim begat Eliezer. Eliezer begat Jose. Jose begat Er. Er begat Elmodad. Elmodad begat Cosam. Cosam begat Addi. Addi begat Melchi. Melchi begat Neri. Neri begat Salathiel. Salathiel begat Zorobabel. Zorobabel begat Rhesa. Rhesa begat Johannan. Johannan begat Juda. Juda begat Joseph. Joseph begat Semei. Semei begat Mattatha. Mattatha begat Maath. Maath begat Nagge. Nagge begat Esli. Esli begat Nahum. Nahum begat Amos. Amos begat Mattîtha. Mattîtha begat Joseph. Joseph begat Janni. Janni begat Melchi. Melchi begat Levi. Levi begat Matthat. Matthat begat Heli. Heli begat Joseph.

Know too, O my brother, that Mattan the son of Eliezer--whose descent was from the family of Solomon--took a wife whose name was Astha (or Essetha) and by her begat Jacob naturally. Mattan died, and Melchi--whose family descended from Nathan the son of David--took her to wife, and begat by her Eli (or Heli); hence Jacob and Heli are brothers, (the sons) of (one) mother. Eli took a wife and died without children. Then Jacob took her to wife, to raise up seed to his brother, according to the command of the law; and he begat by her Joseph, who was the son of Jacob according to nature, but the son of Heli according to the law; so whichever ye choose, whether according to nature, or according to the law, Christ is found to be the son of David. It is moreover right to know that Eliezer begat two sons, Mattan and Jotham. Mattan begat Jacob, and Jacob begat Joseph; Jotham begat Zadok, and Zadok begat Mary. From this it is clear that Joseph's father and Mary's father were cousins.

OF THE ANNUNCIATION OF THE ANGEL TO YÔNÂKÎR (JOACHIM) IN RESPECT OF MARY

THIS Zadok, who was called Yônâkîr, and Dinah his wife were righteous before God, and were rich in earthly riches and in goods and chattels; but they had neither fruit nor offspring like other people[257]. They were reproached by the people for their barrenness, and they did not allow them to offer up the offering except after every one else, because they had no children among the people of Israel. And Yônâkîr went out into the desert, and pitched his tent outside the encampment, and he prayed before God with mournful tears, and put on garments of mourning; so also did Dinah his wife. And God heard their prayers and accepted the sacrifices of their tears. The angel of God came to them, and announced to them the conception of Mary, saying, 'Your prayer has been heard before God, and behold, He will give you blessed fruit, a daughter who shall be a sign and a wonder among all the generations of the world; and all families shall be blessed through her.' Then they two praised God, and Zadok returned to his habitation. And Dinah his wife conceived, and brought forth Mary; and from that day she was called Hannah (Anna) instead of Dinah, for the Lord had had compassion upon her. Now the name 'Mary' (Maryam or Miriam) is interpreted 'lifted up,' 'exalted;' and they rejoiced in her exceedingly. And after six months her parents said to one another, 'We will not allow her to walk upon the ground[258];' and they carried her with sacrifices and offerings, and brought her to the temple of the Lord. And they sacrificed oxen and sheep to the Lord, and offered Mary to the high priest. He laid his hand upon her head, and blessed her, saying, 'Blessed shalt thou be among women.' Two years after she was weaned, they brought her to the temple of the Lord, even as they had vowed to the Lord, and delivered her to the high priest. He laid his hand upon her head, and blessed her, and said to her that she should give herself over to the aged women who were there. And she was brought up with the virgins in the temple of the Lord, and performed the service of the temple with joyful heart and godly fervour until she was twelve years old. Because she was beautiful in appearance, the priests and the high priest took counsel and prayed before God that He would reveal to them what they should do with her[259]. And the angel of God appeared unto the high priest and said to him,

'Gather together the staves of the men who have been left widowers by their first wives, and are well known for piety, uprightness, and righteousness, and what God sheweth thee, do.' And they brought many staves and laid them down in the temple; and they prayed before God that day and its night. The chief priest went into the temple and gave to each of them his staff, and when Joseph took his staff in his hand, there went forth from it a white dove, and hovered over the top of the rod, and sat upon it. The chief priest drew near to Joseph and kissed him on his head, and said to him, 'The blessed maiden has fallen to thy lot from the Lord; take her to thee until she arrives at the age for marriage, and (then) make a marriage feast after the manner and custom of men; for it is meet for thee (to do so) more than others, because ye are cousins.' Joseph said to the chief priest, 'I am an old and feeble man, and this is a girl, and unfit for my aged condition; it is better to give her to one of her own age, because I cannot rely upon myself to watch her and guard her.' The chief priest said to him, 'Take heed that thou dost not transgress the command of God, and bring a punishment upon thee.' So Joseph took Mary, and went to his dwelling-place.

[260]Some days after the priests distributed various coloured silken threads to weave for the veil of the sanctuary; and it fell to Mary's lot to weave purple. And while she was in the temple in prayer, having placed incense before the Lord, suddenly the archangel Gabriel appeared to her in the form of a middle-aged man, and a sweet odour was diffused from him; and Mary was terrified at the sight of the angel.

OF THE ANNUNCIATION BY GABRIEL TO MARY OF THE CONCEPTION OF OUR LORD

AT the ninth hour of the first day of the week, on the twenty-fifth of the month of Adar,--though some say on the first day of the month of Nisan, which is correct,--in the three hundred and seventh year of Alexander the son of Philip, or of Nectanebus[261], the Macedonian, six months after Elizabeth's conception of John, the archangel Gabriel appeared to Mary and said to her, 'Peace be to thee, O full of grace! our Lord is with thee, O blessed among women!' As for her, when she saw (him), she was terrified at his words, and was thinking what this salutation was. The angel said to her, 'Fear not Mary, for thou hast found grace with God. And behold, thou shalt conceive and bear a son, and thou shalt call his name Emmanuel, which is interpreted, "our God is with us." This (child) shall be great, and shall be called the Son of the Highest.' Mary said to the angel, 'Behold, I am the handmaid of the Lord; let it be to me according to thy word.' And the angel went away from her. In those days Mary arose, and went to Elizabeth het cousin, and she went in and saluted Elizabeth. And it came to pass that when Elizabeth heard Mary's salutation, the babe leaped in her womb, and John in Elizabeth's womb bowed down to our Lord in Mary's womb, as a servant to his master. Mary remained with Elizabeth about three months, and then returned to her house. After the lapse of six months, Joseph saw that Mary had conceived, and he was troubled in his mind, and said, 'What answer shall I give to the high priest in respect of this trial which has befallen me?' And because he relied upon the purity of his spouse, he fell into perplexity and doubt, and said to her, 'Whence hast thou this? and who has beguiled thee, O perfect dove? Wast thou not brought up with the pure virgins and venerable matrons in the temple of the Lord?' And she wept, saying, 'As the Lord God liveth, I have never known man nor had connexion with any one;' but she did not speak to him of the angel and the cause of her conception. Then Joseph medi-tated within himself and said, 'If I reveal this matter before men, I fear lest it may be from God; and if I keep it back and hide it, I fear the rebuke and penalty of the law.' For the Jews did not approach their wives until they made a feast to the high priest, and then they took them. And Joseph thought that he would put her away secretly; and while he was pondering these things in his heart, the angel of the Lord appeared to him in a dream, and said, 'Joseph, son of David, fear not to take Mary thy wife; for that which is born in her is of the Holy Spirit.' He spake well when he said 'in her,' and not 'of her.'

And the priests heard of Mary's conception, and they made an accusation against Joseph, as if deceit had been found in him. Joseph said, 'As the Lord liveth, I know not the cause of her conception;' and Mary likewise swore this. There was a custom among the Jews that, when any one of them was accused with an accusation, they made him drink 'the water of trial[262];' if he were innocent, he was not hurt, but if he were guilty, his belly swelled, and his body became swollen, and the mark of chastisement appeared in him. When they had made Mary and Joseph drink of the water of trial, and they were not hurt, the high priest commanded Joseph to guard her diligently until they saw the end of this matter[263].

OF THE BIRTH OF OUR LORD IN THE FLESH

ONE year before the annunciation of our Lord, the emperor of the Romans sent to the land of Palestine Cyrinus[264] the governor, to write down every one for the poll-tax, for the Jews were subject to the empire of the Romans; and every man was written down in his city. And Joseph the carpenter also went up that he might be written down in his city; and by reason of his exceeding great watchfulness for the blessed (Mary), he took her with him upon an ass. When they had gone about three miles, Joseph looked at her and saw that her hand was laid upon her belly, and that her face was contracted with pain; and he thought that she was troubled by the beast, and asked her about her trouble and pain. She said to him, 'Hasten and prepare a place for me to alight, for the pains of childbirth have taken hold upon me.' When he had lifted her down from the animal, he went to fetch a midwife, and found a Hebrew woman whose name was Salome[265]. The heretics say that she was called Hadyôk, but they err from the truth. When Joseph came to the cave, he found it full of brilliant light, and the child wrapped in swaddling clothes and rags, and laid in a crib. And there were shepherds there keeping watch over their flocks, and behold the angel of God came to them, and the glory of the Lord shone upon them; and they feared with an exceeding great fear. The angel said to them, 'Fear not, for behold, I announce to you a great joy which shall be to all the world; for there is born to you this day a Redeemer, who is the Lord Jesus, in the city of David: and this shall be the sign unto you; ye shall find the babe wrapped in swaddling clothes, and laid in a crib.' And suddenly with the angel there appeared many hosts of heaven, praising God and saying, 'Glory to God in the heights, and on earth peace and tranquillity and good hope to men.' And the shepherds went and entered the cave, and they saw as the angel had said to them. The names of the shepherds were these: Asher, Zebulon, Justus, Nicodemus, Joseph, Barshabba, and Jose; seven in number.

THE PROPHECY OF ZÂRÂDÔSHT CONCERNING OUR LORD

THIS Zârâdôsht is Baruch the scribe. When he was sitting by the fountain of water called Glôshâ of Hôrîn, where the royal bath had been erected, he said to his disciples, the king Gûshnâsâph[266] and Sâsân and Mahîmad, 'Hear, my beloved children, for I will reveal to you a mystery concerning the great King who is about to rise upon the world. At the end of time, and at the final dissolution, a child shall be conceived in the womb of a virgin, and shall be formed in her members, without any man approaching her. And he shall be like a tree with beautiful foliage and laden with fruit, standing in a parched land; and the inhabitants of that land shall be gathered together[267] to uproot it from the earth, but shall not be able. Then they will take him and crucify him upon a tree, and heaven and earth shall sit in mourning for his sake; and all the families of the nations shall be in grief for him. He will begin to go down to the depths of the earth, and from the depth he will be exalted to the height; then he will come with the armies of light, and be borne aloft upon white clouds; for he is a child conceived by the Word which establishes natures.' Gûshnâsâph says to him, 'Whence has this one, of whom thou sayest these things, his power? Is he greater than thou, or art thou greater than he?' Zârâdôsht says to him, 'He shall descend from my family; I am he, and he is I; he is in me, and I am in him. When the beginning of his coming appears, mighty signs will be seen in heaven, and his light shall surpass that of the sun. But ye, sons of the seed of life, who have come forth from the treasuries of life and light and spirit, and have been sown in the land of fire and water, for you it is meet to watch and take heed to these things which I have spoken to you, that ye await his coming; for you will be the first to perceive the coming of that great king, whom the prisoners await to be set free. Now, my sons, guard this secret which I have revealed to you, and let it be kept in the treasure-houses of your souls. And when that star rises of which I have spoken, let ambassadors bearing offerings be sent by you, and let them offer worship to him. Watch, and take heed, and despise him not, that he destroy you not with the sword; for he is the king of kings, and all kings receive their crowns from him. He and I are one.' These are the things which were spoken by this second Balaam, and God, according to His custom, compelled him to interpret these things; or he sprang from a people who were acquainted with the prophecies[268] concerning our Lord Jesus Christ, and declared them aforetime.

OF THE STAR WHICH APPEARED IN THE EAST ON THE DAY OF THE BIRTH OF OUR LORD

SOME say that that star appeared to the Magi simultaneously with the birth of our Lord. As for Herod's commanding that all children from two years old and downwards should be slain, it is not as if they required all that length of time for their journey, but they had some accidental delay either in their own country or on the road. Again, Herod did not command that the children should be slain immediately after his having met the Magi, but much time passed in the interval, because he was waiting to hear from them.

The holy Mâr John Chrysostom, in his exposition of Matthew, says, 'The star appeared a long time before[269], for their journey was accomplished with great delay that they might come to the end of it on the day of our Lord's birth. It was meet that He should be worshipped in swaddling bands, that the greatness of the wonder might be recognised; therefore the star appeared to them a long time before. For if the star had appeared to them in the east when He was born in Palestine, they would not have been able to see Him in swaddling bands. Marvel not, if Herod slew the children from two years and downwards, for wrath and fear urged him to increased watchfulness; therefore he added more time than was needful, that no one should be able to escape.'

As touching the nature of that star, whether it was a star in its nature, or in appearance only, it is right to know that it was not of the other stars, but a secret power which appeared like a star; for all the other stars that are in the firmament, and the sun and moon, perform their course from east to west. This one, however, made its course from north to south, for Palestine lies thus, over against Persia. This star was not seen by them at night only, but also during the day, and at noon; and it was seen at the time when the sun is particularly strong, because it was not one of the stars. Now the moon is stronger in its light than all the stars, but it is immediately quenched and its light dissipated by one small ray of the sun. But this star overcame even the beams of the sun by the intensity of its light. Sometimes it appeared, and sometimes it was hidden entirely. It guided the Magi as far as Palestine. When they drew near to Jerusalem, it was hidden; and when they went forth from Herod, and began to journey along the road, it appeared and shewed itself. This was not an ordinary movement of the stars, but a rational power. Moreover, it had no fixed path, but when the Magi travelled, it travelled on also, and when they halted, it also halted; like the pillar of cloud which stopped and went forward when it was convenient for the camp of Israel. The star did not remain always up in the height of heaven, but sometimes it came down and sometimes it mounted up; and it also stood over the head of the Child, as the Evangelist tells us.

OF THE COMING OF THE MAGI FROM PERSIA

WHEN Jesus was born in Bethlehem of Judah, and the star appeared to the Magi in the east, twelve Persian kings took offerings--gold and myrrh and frankincense--and came to worship Him. Their names are these: Zarwândâd the son of Artabân[270], and Hôrmîzdâd the son of Sîtârûk (Santarôk), Gûshnâsâph (Gushnasp) the son of Gûndaphar, and Arshakh the son of Mîhârôk; these four brought gold. Zarwândâd the son of Warzwâd, Îryâhô the son of Kesrô (Khosrau), Artashisht the son of Holîtî, Ashtôn`âbôdan the son of Shîshrôn; these four brought myrrh. Mêhârôk the son of Hûhâm, Ahshîresh the son of Hasbân, Sardâlâh the son of Baladân, Merôdâch the son of Beldarân; these four brought frankincense. Some say that the offerings which the Magi brought and offered to our Lord had been laid in the Cave of Treasures by Adam[271]; and Adam commanded Seth to hand them down from one to another until our Lord rose, and they brought (them), and offered (them) to Him. But this is not received by the Church. When the Magi came to Jerusalem, the whole city was moved; and Herod the king heard it and was moved. And he gathered together the chief priests and the scribes of the people, and enquired about the place in which Christ should be born; and they told him, in Bethlehem of Judah, for so it is written in the prophet[272]. Then Herod called the Magi, and flattered them, and commanded them to seek out the Child diligently, and when they had found Him to tell Herod, that he also might go and worship Him. When the Magi went forth from Herod, and journeyed along the road, the star rose again suddenly, and guided them until it came and stood over (the place) where the Child was. And when they entered the cave, and saw the Child with Mary His mother, they straightway fell down and worshipped Him, and opened their treasures, and offered unto Him offerings, gold and myrrh and frankincense. Gold for His kingship, and myrrh for His burial, and frankincense for His Godhead. And it was revealed to them in a dream that they should not return to Herod, and they went to their land by another way. Some say that the Magi took some of our Lord's swaddling bands with them as a blessed thing[273].

Then Longinus the sage wrote to Augustus Caesar and said to him, 'Magians, kings of Persia, have come and entered thy kingdom, and have offered offerings to a child who is born in Judah; but who he is, and whose son he is, is not known to us.' Augustus Caesar wrote to Longinus, saying, 'Thou hast acted wisely in that thou hast made known to us (these things) and hast not hidden (them) from us.' He wrote also to Herod, and asked him to let him know the story of the Child. When Herod had made enquiries about the Child, and saw that he had been mocked by the Magi, he was wroth, and sent and slew all the children in Bethlehem and its borders, from two years old and downwards, according to the time which he had enquired of the Magi. The number of the children whom he slew was two thousand, but some say one thousand eight hundred. When John[274] the son of Zechariah was sought for, his father took him and brought him before the altar; and he laid his hand upon him, and bestowed on him the priesthood, and then brought him out into the wilderness. When they could not find John, they slew Zechariah his father between the steps[275] and the altar. They say that from the day when Zechariah was slain his blood bubbled up until Titus the son of Vespasian came and slew three hundred myriads of Jerusalem, and then the flow of blood ceased[276]. The father of the child Nathaniel also took him, and wrapped him round, and laid him under a fig-tree; and he was saved from slaughter. Hence our Lord said to Nathaniel, 'Before Philip called thee, I saw thee, when thou wast under the fig-tree.'

OF OUR LORD'S GOING DOWN INTO EGYPT[277]

WHEN the Magi had returned to their country, the angel of the Lord appeared to Joseph in a dream, and said to him, 'Arise, take the Child and His mother, and flee to Egypt; and stay there until I tell thee.' So Joseph arose and took the Child and His mother by night, and fled to Egypt, and was there until the death of Herod. When they were journeying along the road to Egypt, two robbers met them; the name of the one was Titus, that of the other Dûmâchos (?). Dûmâchos wished to harm them and to treat them evilly, but Titus would not let him, and delivered them from the hands of his companion. When they reached the gate of the city called Hermopolis[278], there were by the two buttresses of the gate two figures of brass, that had been made by the sages and philosophers; and they spoke like men. When our Lord and His mother and Joseph entered Egypt, that is to say that city, these two figures cried out with a loud voice, saying, 'A great king has come into Egypt[279].' When the king of Egypt heard this, he was troubled and moved; for he feared lest his kingdom should be taken away from him. And he commanded the heralds to proclaim throughout the whole city, 'If any man knoweth (who He is), let him point (Him) out to us without delay.' When they had made much search and did not find Him, the king commanded all the inhabitants of the city to go outside and come in one by one. When our Lord entered, these two figures cried out, 'This is the king.' And when our Lord was revealed, Pharaoh sought to slay Him. Now Lazarus--whom Christ raised from the dead--was there, and was one of the king's officials, and held in much esteem by the lord of Egypt. He drew near to Joseph and asked them, 'Whence are ye?' They said to him, 'From the land of Palestine.' When he heard that they were from the land of Palestine, he was sorry for them, and came to the king and pledged himself for the Child. And he said to the king, 'O king, live for ever! If deceit be found in this Child, behold, I am before thee, do unto me according to thy will.' This is the (cause) of the love between Lazarus and Christ. One day when Mary was washing the swaddling bands of our Lord, she poured out the water used in washing in a certain place, and there grew up there apûrsam[280] (that is to say balsam) trees, a species of tree not found anywhere else save in this spot in Egypt. Its oil has (divers) properties; if a man dips iron into it, and brings (the iron) near a fire, it shines like wax; if some of it is thrown upon water, it sinks to the bottom; and if a drop of it is dropped upon the hollow of a man's hand, it goes through to the other side. Our Lord remained two years in Egypt, until Herod had died an evil death. He died in this manner. First of all he slew his wife and his daughter, and he killed one man of every family, saying, 'At the time of my death there shall be mourning and weeping and lamentation in the whole city.' His bowels and his legs were swollen with running sores, and matter flowed from them, and he was consumed by worms. He had nine wives and thirteen children. And he commanded his sister Salome and her husband, saying, 'I know that the Jews will hold a great festival on the day of my death; when they are gathered together with the weepers and mourners, slay them, and let them not live after my death.' There was a knife in his hand, and he was eating an apple; and by reason of the severity of his pain, he drew the knife across his throat, and cut it with his own hand; and his belly burst open, and he died and went to perdition. After the death of Herod who slew the children, his son Herod Archelaus reigned, who cut off the head of John. And the angel of the Lord appeared to Joseph in Egypt and said to him, 'Arise, take the Child and His mother, and go to the land of Israel, for those who sought the life of the Child are dead.' So Joseph took the Child and His mother, and came to Galilee; and they dwelt in the city of Nazareth, that what was said in the prophecy might be fulfilled, 'He shall be called a Nazarene.' In the tenth year of the reign of Archelaus the kingdom of the Jews was divided into four parts. To Philip (were assigned) two parts, Ituraea and Trachonitis; to Lysanias one part, which was Abilene; and to Herod the younger the fourth part. And Herod loved Herodias, the wife of his brother Philip.

OF JOHN THE BAPTIST, AND OF THE BAPTISM OF OUR LORD[281]

JOHN the Baptist lived thirty yeats in the desert with the wild beasts; and after thirty years he came from the wilderness to the habitations of men. From the day when his father made him flee to the desert, when he was a child, until he came (again), he covered himself with the same clothes both summer and winter, without changing his ascetic mode of life. And he preached in the wilderness of Judaea, saying, 'Repent, the kingdom of God draweth nigh;' and he baptised them with the baptism of repentance for the remission of their sins. He said to them, 'Behold, there cometh after me a man who is stronger than I, the latchets of whose shoes I am not worthy to unloose. I baptise you with water for repentance, but He who cometh after me is stronger than I; He will baptise you with the Holy Spirit and with fire:' thereby referring to that which was about to be wrought on the apostles, who received the Holy Spirit by tongues of fire, and this took the place of baptism to them, and by this grace they were about to receive all those who were baptised in Christ. Jesus came to John at the river Jordan to be baptised by him; but John restrained Him, saying, 'I need to be baptised by Thee, and art Thou come to me?' Jesus said to him, 'It is meet thus to fulfil the words of prophecy.' When Jesus had been baptised, as soon as He had gone up from the water, He saw that the heavens were rent, and the Spirit like a dove descended upon Him, and a voice from heaven said, 'This is My beloved Son, in whom I am well pleased.' On this day the Trinity was revealed to men; by the Father who cried out, and by the Son who was baptised, and by the Holy Spirit which came down upon Him in the corporeal form of a dove. Touching the voice which was heard from heaven, saying, 'This is My beloved Son, in whom I am well pleased, hear ye Him,' every one heard the voice; but John only was worthy to see the vision of the Spirit by the mind. The day of our Lord's birth was the fourth day of the week, but the day of His baptism was the fifth. When John rebuked Herod, saying that it was not lawful for him to take his brother Philip's wife, he seized John, and cast him into the prison called Machaerûs[282]. And it came to pass on a certain day, when Herod on his birthday made a feast for his nobles, that Bôzîyâ, the daughter of Herodias, came in and danced before the guests; and she was pleasing in the sight of Herod and his nobles. And he said to her, 'Ask of me whatsoever thou desirest and I will give it to thee;' and he sware to her saying that whatever she asked he would give it to her, unto the half of his kingdom. She then went in to Herodias her mother and said to her, 'What shall I ask of him?' She said to her, 'The head of John the Baptist;' for the wretched woman thought that when John should be slain, she and her daughter would be free from the reprover, and would have an opportunity to indulge their lust: for Herod committed adultery with the mother and with her daughter. Then she went in to the king's presence and said to him, 'Give me now the head of John the Baptist on a charger.' And the king shewed sorrow, as if, forsooth, he was not delighted at the murder of the saint; but by reason of the force and compulsion of the oath he was obliged to cut off John's head. If, O wretched Herod, she had demanded of thee the half of thy kingdom, that she might sit upon the throne beside thee and divide (it) with thee, wouldst thou have acceded to her, and not have falsified thy oath, O crafty one? And the king commanded an executioner, and he cut off the head of the blessed man, and he put it in a charger and brought and gave it to the damsel, and the damsel gave it to her mother. Then she went out to dance upon the ice, and it opened under her, and she sank into the water up to her neck; and no one was able to deliver her. And they brought the sword with which John's head had been cut off, and cut off hers and carried it to Herodias her mother. When she saw her daughter's head and that of the holy man, she became blind, and her right hand, with which she had taken up John's head, dried up; and her tongue dried up, because she had reviled him, and Satan entered into her, and she was bound with fetters. Some say that the daughter of Herodias was called Bôzîyâ, but others say that she also was called by her mother's name Herodias. When John was slain, his disciples came and took his body and laid him in a grave; and they came and told Jesus. The two disciples whom John sent to our Lord, saying, 'Art thou He that should come, or do we look for another[283],' were Stephen the martyr and deacon, and Hananyah (Ananias) who baptised Paul. Some say that the wild honey and locusts, which he fed upon in the wilderness, was manna,--which was the food of the children of Israel, and of which Enoch and Elijah eat in Paradise,--for its taste is like that of honey. Moses compares it to coriander seed[284], and the anchorites in the mountains feed upon it. Others say that it was a root like unto a carrot[285]; it is called Kâmûs, and its taste is sweet like honey-comb. Others say that the locusts were in reality some of those which exist in the world, and that the honey-comb was that which is woven by the little bees, and is found in small white cakes in desert places.

OF OUR LORD'S FAST; OF THE STRIFE WHICH HE WAGED WITH THE DEVIL[286]; AND OF THE MIGHTY DEEDS THAT HE WROUGHT

TWO days after His baptism, He chose eight of the twelve disciples; and on the third day He changed the water into wine in the city of Cana. After He went forth from the wilderness, He completed the number of the twelve, according to the number of the tribes of the children of Israel and according to the number of the months. After the twelve disciples, He chose seventy and two, according to the number of the seventy-two elders. When He went out to the desert after He had changed the water into wine, He fasted forty days and forty nights. Some say that our Lord and the devil were waging war with one another for forty days; others say that the three contests took place in one day. After He had conquered the devil by the power of His Godhead, and had given us power to conquer him, He began to teach the nations. He wrought miracles, healed the sick, cleansed the lepers, cast out devils, opened the eyes of the blind, made the lame walk, made cripples stand, gave hearing to the deaf, and speech of tongue to the dumb. He satisfied five thousand with five loaves, and there remained twelve basketfuls; and with seven loaves and two fishes He satisfied four thousand (men), besides women and children, and there remained seven basketfuls. And some writers say that our Lord satisfied forty thousand men and women and children with five loaves. He walked upon the water and the sea as upon dry land. He rebuked the sea when it was disturbed, and it ceased from its disturbance. He raised up four dead; the daughter of Jairus, the widow's son, the servant of the centurion, and His friend Lazarus after (he had been dead) four days. He subjected Himself to the ancient law of Moses, that it might not be thought He was opposed to the divine commandments; and when the time came for Him to suffer, and to draw nigh to death that He might make us live by His death, and to slay sin in His flesh, and to fulfil the prophecies concerning Him, first of all He kept the Passover of the law; He dissolved the old covenant, and then He laid the foundation for the new law by His own Passover.

OF THE PASSOVER OF OUR LORD[287]

WHEN the time of the Passover came, He sent two of His disciples to a man with whom they were not acquainted, saying, 'When ye enter the city, behold, there will meet you a man carrying a pitcher of water; follow him, and wheresoever he entereth, say ye to the master of the house, "Our Master saith, Where is the guest-chamber, where I may eat the Passover with My disciples?" and behold, he will shew a large upper chamber made ready and prepared; there make ye ready for us.' And because at that time crowds of people were flocking thickly into Jerusalem to keep the feast of the Passover, so that all the houses of the inhabitants of Jerusalem were filled with people by reason of the great crowd which was resorting thither, our Lord, by the power of His Godhead, worked upon the master of the house to make ready a large upper chamber without his being aware for whom he was preparing it, but he thought that perhaps some great man among the nobles and grandees of the Jews was about to come to him, and that it was right to keep a room for him furnished with all things (needful); because all those who came from other places to Jerusalem were received into their houses by the people of the city, and whatsoever they required for the use of the feast of the Passover they supplied. Hence the master of the house made ready that upper chamber with all things (needful), and permitted no man to enter therein, being restrained by the power of our Lord. Because a mystical thing was about to be done in it, it was not meet for Him to perform the hidden mystery when others were near. Mâr Basil says: 'On the eve of the Passion, after the disciples had received the body and blood of our Lord, He poured water into a basin and began to wash the feet of His disciples; this was baptism to the apostles. They were not all made perfect, because they were not all pure, for Judas, the son of perdition, was not sanctified[288]; and because that basin of washing was in truth baptism, as our Lord said to Simon Peter, "If I wash thee not, thou hast no part with Me," that is to say, "If I baptise thee not, thou art not able to enter into the kingdom of heaven." Therefore, every one who is not baptised by the priests, and receives not the body and blood of Christ our Lord, enters not into the kingdom of heaven.' Mâr Dâd-îshô` says in his commentary on Abbâ Isaiah[289]: 'When our Lord at the Passover had washed the feet of His disciples, He kissed the knees of Judas, and wiped the soles of his feet with the napkin which was girt round His loins, like a common slave; for everything which our Lord did, He did for our teaching.' Mâr Basil in his 'Questions' advises Christians to eat oil, drink wine, and break their fast on this evening; for in it was the old covenant finished, and the new one inaugurated; and in it was the (chosen) people stripped of holiness, and the nations were sanctified and pardoned. Although this saint permits (this), yet the other fathers do not give leave (to do) this, neither do we, nor those of our confession.

OF THE PASSION OF OUR LORD

THREE years and three months after His baptism, Judas Iscariot the son of Simon betrayed his Lord to death. He was called Iscariot (Sekhariôtâ) from the name of his town (Sekhariôt), and he had the sixth place among the disciples before he betrayed our Lord. Our Lord was crucified at the third hour of Friday, the ninth of Nisan. Caiaphas, who condemned our Lord, is Josephus. The name of Bar-Abbâ was Jesus[290]. The name of the soldier who pierced our Lord with the spear, and spat in His face, and smote Him on His cheek, was Longinus; it was he who lay upon a sick bed for thirty-eight years, and our Lord healed him, and said to him, 'Behold, thou art healed; sin no more, lest something worse than the first befall thee[291].' The watchers at the grave were five, and these are their names: Issachar, Gad, Matthias, Barnabas and Simon; but others say they were fifteen, three centurions and their Roman and Jewish soldiers. Some men have a tradition that the stone which was laid upon the grave of our Lord was the stone which poured out water for the children of Israel in the wilderness. The grave in which our Redeemer was laid was prepared for Joshua the son of Nun, and was carefully guarded by the Divine will for the burial of our Lord. The purple which they put on our Lord mockingly, was given in a present to the Maccabees by the emperors of the Greeks; and they handed it over to the priests for dressing the temple[292]. The priests took it and brought it to Pilate, testifying and saying, 'See the purple which He prepared when He thought to become king,' The garment which the soldiers divided into four parts indicates the passibility of His body, The robe without seam at the upper end which was not rent, is the mystery of the Godhead which cannot admit suffering. As touching the blood and water which came forth from His side[293], John the son of Zebedee was deemed worthy to see that vivifying flow from the life-giving fountain. Mâr John Chrysostom says: 'When His side was rent by the soldiers with the spear, there came forth immediately water and blood. The water is a type of baptism, and the blood is the mystery of His precious blood, for baptism was given first, and then the cup of redemption. But in the gospel it is written, "There went forth blood and water[294],"' As to the tree upon which our Redeemer was crucified, some have said that He was crucified upon those bars with which they carried the ark of the covenant; and others that it was upon the wood of the tree on which Abraham offered up the ram as an offering instead of Isaac. His hands were nailed upon the wood of the fig-tree of which Adam ate, and behold, we have mentioned its history with that of Moses' rod. The thirty pieces of silver (zûzê) which Judas received, and for which he sold his Lord, were thirty pieces according to the weight of the sanctuary, and were equal to six hundred pieces according to the weight of our country[295]. Terah[296] made these pieces for Abraham his son; Abraham gave them to Isaac; Isaac bought a village with them; the owner of the village carried them to Pharaoh; Pharaoh sent them to Solomon the son of David for the building of his temple; and Solomon took them and placed them round about the door of the altar. When Nebuchadnezzar came and took captive the children of Israel, and went into Solomon's temple and saw that these pieces were beautiful, he took them, and brought them to Babylon with the captives of the children of Israel. There were some Persian youths there as hostages, and when Nebuchadnezzar came from Jerusalem, they sent to him everything that was meet for kings and rulers. And since gifts and presents had been sent by the Persians, he released their sons and gave them gifts and presents, among which were those pieces of silver about which we have spoken; and they carried them to their parents. When Christ was born and they saw the star, they arose and took those pieces of silver and gold and myrrh and frankincense, and set out on the journey; and they came to the neighbourhood of Edessa, and these kings fell asleep by the roadside. And they arose and left the pieces behind them, and did not remember them, but forgot that anything of theirs remained behind. And certain merchants came and found them, and took these pieces, and came to the neighbourhood of Edessa, and sat down by a well of water. On that very day an angel came to the shepherds, and gave them the garment without seam at the upper end, woven throughout. And he said to them, 'Take this garment, in which is the life of mankind.' And the shepherds took the garment, and came to the well of water by the side of which were those merchants. They said to them, 'We have a garment without seam at the upper end; will ye buy it?' The merchants said to them, 'Bring it here.' When they saw the garment, they marvelled and said to the shepherds: 'We have thirty pieces of silver which are meet for kings; take them and give us this garment.' When the merchants had taken the garment, and had gone into the city of Edessa, Abgar the king sent to them and said, 'Have ye anything meet for kings, that I may buy it from you?' The merchants said to him, 'We have a garment without seam at the upper end.' When the king saw the garment, he said to them, 'Whence have ye this garment?' They said to him, 'We came to a well by the gate of thy city, and we saw it in the hands of some shepherds, and we bought it from them for thirty pieces of stamped silver, which were also meet for kings like thyself.' The king sent for the shepherds, and took the pieces from them, and sent them together with the garment to Christ for the good that He had done him in healing his sickness. When Christ saw the garment and the pieces, He kept the garment by Him, but He sent the pieces to the Jewish treasury. When Judas Iscariot came to the chief priests and said to them, 'What will ye give me that I may deliver Him to you?' the priests arose and brought those pieces, and gave them to Judas Iscariot; and when he repented, he returned them to the Jews, and went and hanged himself. And the priests took them and bought with them a field for a burial-place for strangers.

[297]Of Joseph the senator (βουλευτής {Greek: Bouleuths}), and why he was thus called. The senators were a class very much honoured in the land of the Romans; and if it happened that no one could be found of the royal lineage, they made a king from among this class. If one of them committed an offence, they used to beat his horse with white woollen gloves instead of him. This Joseph was not a senator by birth, but he purchased the dignity, and enrolled himself among the Roman senate, and was called Senator[298].

[299]As for the committal of Mary to John the son of Zebedee by our Lord, He said to her, 'Woman, behold thy son;' and to John He said, 'Behold thy mother;' and from that hour he took her into his house and ministered unto her. Mary lived twelve years[300] after our Lord's Ascension: the sum of the years which she lived in the world was fifty-eight years, but others say sixty-one years[301]. She was not buried on earth, but the angels carried her to Paradise, and angels bore her bier. On the day of her death all the apostles were gathered together, and they prayed over her and were blessed by her[302]. Thomas was in India, and an angel took him up and brought him, and he found the angels carrying her bier through the air; and they brought it nigh to Thomas, and he also prayed and was blessed by her.

[303]As regards the name of ʿarûbhtâ (i.e. the eve of the Jewish Sabbath), it was not known until this time, but that day was called the sixth day. And when the sun became dark, and the Divine Care also set and abandoned the Israelitish people, then that day was called ʿarûbhtâ.

Touching the writing which was written in Greek, Hebrew and Latin, and set over Christ's head, there was no Aramean written upon the tablet, for the Arameans or Syrians had no part in (the shedding of) Christ's blood, but only the Greeks and Hebrews and Romans; Herod the Greek and Caiaphas the Hebrew and Pilate the Roman. Hence when Abgar the Aramean king of Mesopotamia heard (of it), he was wroth against the Hebrews and sought to destroy them.

OF THE RESURRECTION OF OUR LORD

SINCE the history of our Lord's Passion and Resurrection is recorded in the Gospel, there is no need to repeat it (here). After our Lord rose from the dead, He appeared ten times. First, to Mary Magdalene, as John the Evangelist records[304]. Secondly, to the women at the grave, as Matthew mentions[305]. Thirdly, to Cleopas and his companion, as Luke says[306]. The companion of Cleopas, when they were going to Emmaus, was Luke the Evangelist. Fourthly, to Simon Peter, as Luke says[307]. Fifthly, to all the disciples, except Thomas, on the evening of the first day of the week, when he went in through the closed doors, as Luke and John say[308]. Sixthly, eight days after, to the disciples, and to Thomas with them, as John says[309]. Seventhly, on the mount, as Matthew says[310]. Eighthly, upon the sea of Tiberias, as John says[311]. The reason that Simon Peter did not recognise Him was because he had denied Him, and was ashamed to look upon Him; but John, because of his frank intimacy with our Lord, immediately that he saw Him, knew Him. Ninthly, when He was taken up to heaven from the Mount of Olives, as Mark and Luke say[312]. Tenthly, to the five hundred at once, who had risen from the dead, as Paul says[313]. After His Ascension, He appeared to Paul on the way to Damascus, when He blinded his eyes[314]; and also to Stephen, the martyr and deacon, when he was stoned[315].

OF THE ASCENSION OF OUR LORD TO HEAVEN

AFTER our Redeemer had risen from the grave, and had gone about in the world forty days, He appeared to His disciples ten times, and ate and drank with them by the side of the Sea of Tiberias. At this point the heathen say to us, that if our Lord really ate and drank after His resurrection, there will certainly be eating and drinking after (our) resurrection; but if He did not really eat and drink, then all the actions of Christ are mere phantasms. To these we make answer, that this world is a world of need for food; therefore He ate and drank, that it might not be thought He was a phantom; and because many who have risen from the dead have eaten and drunk in (this) world until they departed and died, as, for example, the dead (child) whom Elisha raised, and the dead whom our Lord raised. Our Lord did not eat after His resurrection because He needed food, but only to make certain His humanity: for, behold[316], He once remained in the desert forty days without food, and was not injured by hunger. Some say that after His resurrection our Lord ate food like unto that which the angels ate in the house of Abraham, and that the food was dissipated and consumed by the Divine Power, just as fire licks up oil without any of it entering into its substance. Our Lord remained upon the earth forty days, even as He had fasted forty days, and as Elijah fasted forty days, and as Moses fasted forty days at two several times, and as the rain continued for forty days during the flood, and as God admonished the Ninevites for forty days, and as the spies remained (absent) for forty days, and as the children of Israel wandered about in the wilderness for forty years, and like the child whose fashioning in the womb is completed in forty days. After forty days, our Lord took up His disciples to the Mount of Olives, and laid His hand upon them, and blessed them, and commanded them concerning the preaching and teaching of the nations. And it came to pass that while He was blessing them, He was separated from them, and went up to heaven; and they worshipped Him. And there appeared to them angels, encouraging them and saying, 'This Jesus, who has been taken up from you to heaven, is about to come again even as ye have seen Him go up to heaven.' Then they returned to that upper chamber where they were, and stayed there ten days, until they received the Holy Spirit in the form of tongues of fire. Simon Peter said to his fellow-disciples, 'It is right for us to put some one in the place of Judas to complete the number of twelve;' and they cast lots, and the lot fell upon Matthias, and he was numbered with the eleven apostles[317].

As concerning the manner in which our Lord entered heaven without cleaving it, some say that He went in as He did through the closed doors; and as He came forth from the virgin womb, and Mary's virginity returned to its former state; and like the sweat from the body; and as water is taken up by the roots of the olive and other trees, and reaches in the twinkling of an eye the leaves, flowers and fruits, as if through certain ducts, without holes or channels being pierced in them. Thus by an infinite and ineffable miracle our Lord entered into heaven without cleaving it. And if the bodies of us who are accustomed to drink water and wine pour out sweat without our flesh being rent or our skin pierced, how very much easier is it for the Divine Power to go in through closed doors and within the firmament of heaven without rending or cleaving it?

[318]As regards the upper chamber in which our Lord held His Passover, some say that it belonged to Lazarus, and others to Simon the Cyrenian, and others to Joseph the senator; but Joshua the son of Nun, the Catholicus[319], says that it belonged to Nicodemus. The apostles remained in the upper chamber ten days after the Ascension, being constant in fasting and prayer, and expecting the Spirit, the Comforter, which our Lord Jesus Christ promised them.

OF THE DESCENT OF THE HOLY SPIRIT UPON THE APOSTLES IN THE UPPER CHAMBER

TEN days after our Lord's Ascension, when the holy apostles were assembled in the upper chamber waiting for the promise of our Lord, of a sudden, at the third hour of the holy Sunday of Pentecost, a mighty sound was heard, so that all men were terrified and marvelled at the mightiness of the sound; and the chamber was filled with an ineffably strong light. And there appeared over the head of each one of them (something) in the form of tongues of fire, and there breathed forth from thence a sweet odour which surpassed all aromas in this world. The eyes of their hearts were opened, and they began interpreting new things and uttering wonderful things in the languages of all nations. When the Jews saw them, they thought within themselves that they had been drinking new wine and were drunk, and that their minds were depraved. On that day they participated in the mystery of the body and blood of our Lord, and sanctified the leavened bread of the sign of the cross (the eucharistic wafers) and the oil of baptism.

Some men have a tradition that when our Lord broke His body for His disciples in the upper chamber, John the son of Zebedee hid a part of his portion until our Lord rose from the dead. And when our Lord appeared to His disciples and to Thomas with them, He said to Thomas, 'Hither with thy finger and lay it on My side, and be not unbelieving, but believing.' Thomas put his finger near to our Lord's side, and it rested upon the mark of the spear, and the disciples saw the blood from the marks of the spear and nails. And John took that piece of consecrated bread, and wiped up that blood with it; and the Easterns, Mâr Addai and Mâr Mârî, took that piece, and with it they sanctified this unleavened bread which has been handed down among us[320]. The other disciples did not take any of it, because they said, 'We will consecrate for ourselves whenever we wish.' As for the oil or baptism, some say that it was part of the oil with which they anointed the kings; others say that it was part of the unguent wherewith they embalmed our Lord; and many agree with this (statement). Others again say that when John took that piece of consecrated bread of the Passover in his hand, it burst into flame and burnt in the palm of his hand, and the palm of his hand sweated, and he took that sweat and hid it for the sign of the cross of baptism. This account we have heard by ear from the mouth of a recluse and visitor (περιοδευτής {Greek: periodeuths}), and we have not received it from Scripture. The word Pentecost is interpreted 'the completion of fifty days.'

OF THE TEACHING OF THE APOSTLES, AND OF THE PLACES OF EACH ONE OF THEM, AND OF THEIR DEATHS[321]

NEXT we write the excellent discourse composed by Mâr Eusebius of Caesarea upon the places and families of the holy apostles.

Know then that the apostles were twelve and seventy. When the apostles had received the gift of the Holy Spirit, on the day following they fasted this feast of the apostles (which we keep)[322]; but the Malkâyê (Melchites)[323] say that the apostles fasted eight days after. Their names are as follows.

Simon, the chief of the apostles, was from Bethsaida, of the tribe of Naphtali. He first preached in Antioch, and built there the first of all churches, which was in the house of Cassianus, whose son he restored to life. He remained there one year, and there the disciples were called Christians. From thence he went to Rome, where he remained for twenty-seven years; and in the three hundred and seventy-sixth year of the Greeks, the wicked Nero crucified him head downwards.

Andrew his brother preached in Scythia and Nicomedia and Achaia. He built a church in Byzantium, and there he died and was buried.

John the son of Zebedee (Zabhdai) was also from Bethsaida, of the tribe of Zebulun. He first preached in Asia (Ephesus), and was afterwards cast into exile in the island of Patmos by Tiberius Caesar. He then went to Ephesus, and built in it a church. Three of his disciples went with him: Ignatius, who was afterwards bishop of Antioch, and who was thrown to the beasts in Rome; Polycarp, who was afterwards bishop of Smyrna, and was crowned by fire; and John, to whom he committed the priesthood and the bishopric after him. When John had lived a long time, he died and was buried at Ephesus; and John, the disciple of the Evangelist, who became bishop of Ephesus, buried him[324]; for he commanded them that no one should know the place of his burial. The graves of both of them are in Ephesus; the hidden one of the Evangelist, and the other of his disciple John, the author of the Revelation; he said that everything he had written down, he had heard from John the Evangelist.

James, the brother of John, preached in his city Bethsaida, and built a church there. Herod Agrippas slew him with the sword one year after the Ascension of our Lord. He was laid in Âkâr, a city of Marmârîkâ[325].

Philip also was from Bethsaida, of the tribe of Asher. He preached in Phrygia, Pamphylia and Pisidia; he built a church in Pisidia, and died and was buried there. He lived twenty-seven years as an apostle[326].

Thomas was from Jerusalem, of the tribe of Judah. He taught the Parthians, Medes and Indians[327]; and because he baptised the daughter of the king of the Indians, he stabbed him with a spear and he died[328]. Habbân the merchant brought his body, and laid it in Edessa, the blessed city of Christ our Lord[329]. Others say that he was buried in Mahlûph, a city in the land of the Indians[330].

Matthew the Evangelist was from Nazareth, of the tribe of Issachar. He preached in Palestine, Tyre and Sidon, and went as far as Gabbûlâ[331]. He died and was buried in Antioch, a city of Pisidia[332].

Bartholomew was from Endor, of the tribe of Issachar. He preached in inner Armenia, Ardeshîr[333], Ketarbôl[334], Radbîn, and Prûharmân. After he had lived thirty years as an apostle, Hûrstî[335] the king of the Armenians crucified him, and he was buried in the church which he built in Armenia.

Jude, the son of James, who was surnamed Thaddaeus (Taddai), who is also Lebbaeus (Lebbai), was from Jerusalem, of the tribe of Judah. He preached in Laodicea and in Antaradus and Arwâd[336]. He was stoned in Arwâd, and died and was buried there[337].

Simon Zelôtes was from Galilee, of the tribe of Ephraim. He preached in Shemêshât (Samosâta), Pârîn (Perrhê), Zeugma, Hâlâb (Aleppo), Mabbôg (Manbig), and Kenneshrîn (Kinnesrîn). He built a church in Kyrrhos, and died and was buried there[338].

James, the son of Alphaeus (Halphai), was from the Jordan, of the tribe of Manasseh. He preached in Tadmor (Palmyra), Kirkêsion (Kirkîsiyâ), and

Callinîcos (ar-Rakkah), and came to Batnân of Serûg (Sarûg), where he built a church, and died and was buried there[339].

Judas Iscariot, the betrayer, was from the town of Sekharyût of the tribe of Gad, though some say that he was of the tribe of Dan. He was like unto the serpent that acts deceitfully towards its master, because like a serpent, he dealt craftily with his Lord. Matthias, of the tribe of Reuben, came in in his stead. He preached in Hellas, and in Sicily, where he built a church, and died and was buried in it[340].

While James the brother of our Lord was teaching the Jews in Jerusalem, they cast him down from a pinnacle of the temple; and while his life was yet in him, a fuller of cloth smote him upon the head with a club and beat it in; and afterwards they stoned him with stones[341].

John the Baptist was of the tribe of Levi. Herod the tetrarch slew him, and his body was laid in Sebastia.

Ananias (Hananyâ) the disciple of the Baptist taught in Damascus and Arbêl[342]. He was slain by Pôl, the general of the army of Aretas[343], and was laid in the church which he built at Arbêl (Irbil).

Paul of Tarsus was a Pharisee by sect, of the tribe of Ephraim[344]. When he had been baptised by Ananias, he wrought many miracles, and taught great cities, and bore and suffered dangers not a few for the name of Christ. Afterwards he went to Peter at Rome. When they divided the world between them, and the heathen fell to Paul's lot, and the Jewish nation to Peter, and they had turned[345] many to the truth of Christ, Nero commanded that they should both die a cruel death. Then Simon asked to be crucified head downwards, that he might kiss that part of the cross where the heels of his Master had been. As they were going forth to be slain, they gave the laying on of hands of the priesthood to their disciples, Peter to Mark, and Paul to Luke. When Peter had been crucified, and Paul slain, together with many of those who had become their disciples, Mark and Luke went forth by night, and brought their bodies into the city. Now Paul's head was lost among the slain, and could not be found. Some time after, when a shepherd was passing by the spot where the slain were buried, he found Paul's head, and took it upon the top of his staff, and laid it by his sheep-fold. At night he saw a fire blazing over it, and he went in (to the city) and informed the holy bishop Xystus (Sixtus) and the clergy of the church; and they all recognised that it was Paul's head. Xystus said to them, 'Let us watch and pray the whole night, and let us bring out the body and lay the head at its feet; and if it joins again to its neck, it will be certain that it is Paul's.' And when they had done so, the whole body was restored, and the head was joined to its neck as if the vertebrae had never been severed; and those who saw it were amazed and glorified God. From his call to the end of his life was thirty-five years; he went about in every place for thirty-one years; for two years he was in prison at Caesarea, and for two years at Rome. He was martyred in the thirty-sixth year after the Passion of our Lord, and was laid with great honour in the magnificent royal catacombs in Rome. They celebrate every year the day of his commemoration on the twenty-ninth of the month of Tammûz[346].

Luke the physician and Evangelist was first of all a disciple of Lazarus, the brother of Mary and Martha, and was afterwards baptised by Philip in the city of Beroea[347]. He was crowned with the sword by Hôros[348], the judge (or governor) of the emperor Tiberius, while he was preaching in Alexandria, and was buried there.

Mark the Evangelist preached in Rome, and died and was buried there[349]. Some say that he was the son of Simon Peter's wife, others that he was the Son of Simon; and Rhoda was his sister. He was first called John, but the Apostles changed his name and called him Mark, that there might not be two Evangelists of one name.

Addai was from Paneas, and he preached in Edessa and in Mesopotamia in the days of Abgar the king; and he built a church in Edessa. After Abgar died, Herod[350] Abgar's son slew him in the fortress of Aggêl[351]. His body was afterwards taken and carried to Rome; but some say that he was laid in Edessa.

Aggai his disciple was first of all a maker of silks for Abgar, and became a disciple. After Abgar's death, his son reigned, and he required of Aggai to weave silks for him; and when he consented not, saying, 'I cannot forsake teaching and preaching to return to weaving,' he smote him with a club upon his legs and brake them, and he died[352].

Thaddaeus (Taddai) came after him at Edessa, and Herod, the son of Abgar, slew him also; he was buried at Edessa.

Zacchaeus (Zaccai) the publican[353] and the young man whom our Lord brought to life were both slain together while they were preaching in Mount Hôrôn.

The Jews smote Simon the leper while he was teaching in Ramah, and he died (there).

Joseph the Senator taught in Galilee and Decapolis; he was buried in his town of Ramah.

Nicodemus the Pharisee, the friend of our Lord, received and honoured the Apostles in Jerusalem; and he died and was buried there[354].

Nathaniel was stoned while he was teaching in Mount Hôrôn[355], and died.

Simon the Cyrenian was slain while he was teaching in the island of Chios.

Simon the son of Cleopas became bishop of Jerusalem. When he was an old man, one hundred years of age, Irenaeus the chiliarch crucified him.

Stephen the martyr was stoned with stones at Jerusalem, and his body was laid in the village of Kephar Gamlâ.

Mark, who was surnamed John, taught at Nyssa and Nazianzus. He built a church at Nazianzus, and died and was buried there. Some say that he is the Evangelist, as we have mentioned.

Cephas, whom Paul mentions[356], taught in Baalbec, Hims (Emesa) and Nathrôn (Batharûn). He died and was buried in Shîrâz[357].

Barnabas taught in Italy and in Kûrâ; he died and was buried in Samos[358].

Titus taught in Crete, and there he died and was buried[359].

Sosthenes taught in the country of Pontus and Asia. He was thrown into the sea by the command of Nonnus the prefect.

Criscus (Crescens) taught in Dalmatia; he was imprisoned in Alexandria, where he died of hunger and was buried.

Justus taught in Tiberias and in Caesarea, where he died and was buried.

Andronicus taught in Illyricum, where he died and was buried.

The people of Zeugma slew Rufus while he was teaching in Zeugma.

Patrobas taught in Chalcedon, and he died and was buried there.

Hermas the shepherd taught in Antioch, and he died and was buried there.

Narcissus taught in Hellas, and he died and was buried there[360].

Asyncritus went to Beth-Hûzâyê (Khûzistân)[361], and there he died and was buried.

Aristobulus taught in Isauria, and there he died and was buried.

Onesimus[362] was the slave of Philemon, and he fled from him and went to Paul, while he was in prison; because of this Paul calls him 'the son whom I have begotten in my bonds.' His legs were broken in Rome.

Apollos the elect was burnt with fire by Sparacleus (?), the governor of Gangra.

Olympas, Stachys and Stephen were imprisoned in Tarsus, and there they died in prison.

Junias was captured in Samos, and there he was slain and died.

Theocritus died while teaching in Ilios, and was buried there.

Martalus (?) was slain while teaching the barbarians.

Niger taught in Antioch, and died and was buried there.

They dragged Lucius[363] behind a horse, and thus he ended his life.

While Alexander was teaching in Heracleôpolis, they threw him into a pit and he died.

Milus[364], while he was teaching in Rhodes, was thrown into the sea and drowned.

Silvanus and Hêrôdiôn (Rhôdiôn) were slain while they were preaching in the city of Accô.

Silas[365] taught in Sarapolis (Hierapolis ?), and died and was buried there.

Timothy taught in Ephesus, and died and was buried there.

Manael was burnt with fire while teaching in Accô, and died.

The Eunuch whom Philip baptised, the officer of Candace the queen of the Ethiopians, went to Ethiopia and preached there. Afterwards, while he was preaching in the island of Parparchia (?), they strangled him with a cord.

Jason[366] and Sosipatrus were thrown to the wild beasts while they were teaching in Olmius (?).

Demas taught in Thessalonica, and there he died and was buried.

Omius (Hymenaeus) taught in Melitene, and there he died and was buried.

They threw Thraseus into a fiery furnace, while he was teaching at Laodicea.

Bistorius (Aristarchus ?) taught in the island of Kô, and there he died and was buried.

Abrios (?) and Môtos (?)[367] went to the country of the Ethiopians, and there they died and were buried.

Levi was slain by Charmus[368], while he was teaching in Paneas.

Nicetianus (Nicetas) was sawn in two while teaching in Tiberias[369].

While John and Theodorus were preaching in the theatre of Baalbec, they threw them to the beasts.

The prefect Methalius (?) slew Euchestion (?) and Simon in Byzantium.

Ephraim (Aphrem) taught in Baishân, and he died and was buried there.

Justus was slain at Corinth.

James taught and preached in Nicomedia, and he died and was buried there.

THE NAMES OF THE APOSTLES IN ORDER[370]

THE names of the twelve. Simon Peter; Andrew his brother; James the son of Zebedee; John his brother; Philip; Bartholomew; Thomas; Matthew the publican; James the son of Alphaeus; Labbaeus, who was surnamed Thaddaeus; Simon the Cananite; Judas Iscariot, in whose stead came in Matthias.

The names of the seventy[371]. James, the son of Joseph; Simon the son of Cleopas; Cleopas his father; Joses; Simon; Judah; Barnabas; Manaeus (?); Ananias, who baptised Paul; Cephas, who preached at Antioch; Joseph the senator; Nicodemus the archon; Nathaniel the chief scribe; Justus, that is Joseph, who is called Barshabbâ; Silas; Judah; John, surnamed Mark; Mnason, who received Paul; Manaël, the foster-brother of Herod; Simon called Niger; Jason[372], who is (mentioned) in the Acts (of the Apostles); Rufus[373]; Alexander; Simon the Cyrenian, their father; Lucius the Cyrenian; another Judah, who is mentioned in the Acts (of the Apostles); Judah, who is called Simon; Eurion (Orion) the splay-footed; Thôrus (?); Thorîsus (?); Zabdon; Zakron. These are the seven[374] who were chosen with Stephen: Philip the Evangelist, who had three[375] daughters that used to prophesy; Stephen; Prochorus; Nicanor; Timon; Parmenas; Nicolaus[376], the Antiochian proselyte; Andronicus[377] the Greek; Titus; Timothy.

These are the five who were with Peter in Rome: Hermas; Plîgtâ; Patrobas; Asyncritus; Hermas.

These are the six[378] who came with Peter to Cornelius: Criscus[379] (Crescens); Milichus; Kîrîtôn (Crito); Simon; Gaius, who received Paul; Abrazon (?); Apollos.

These are the twelve who were rejected from among the seventy, as Judas Iscariot was from among the twelve, because they absolutely denied our Lord's divinity at the instigation of Cerinthus. Of these Luke said, 'They went out from us, but they were not of us[380];' and Paul called them 'false apostles and deceitful workers[381].' Simon; Levi; Bar-Kubbâ; Cleon; Hymenaeus; Candarus[382]; Clithon (?); Demas; Narcissus; Slîkîspus (?); Thaddaeus;

Mârûthâ. In their stead there came in these: Luke the physician; Apollos the elect; Ampelius; Urbanus; Stachys; Popillius (or Publius)[383]; Aristobulus; Stephen (not the Corinthian); Herodion the son of Narcissus; Olympas; Mark the Evangelist; Addai; Aggai; Mâr Mâri.

It is said that each one of the twelve and of the seventy wrote a Gospel; but in order that there might be no contention and that the number of 'Acts' might not be multiplied, the apostles adopted a plan and chose two of the seventy, Luke and Mark, and two of the twelve, Matthew and John.

OF SOME MINOR MATTERS

THESE are they who were married among the apostles: Peter, the chief of the apostles; Philip the Evangelist; Paul; Nathaniel, who is Bartholomew; Labbaeus, who is Thaddaeus, who is Judah the son of Jacob; Simon the Cananite, who is Zelotes, who is Judah the son of Simon.

The child whom our Lord called and set (in the midst), and said, 'Except ye be converted, and become as children, ye shall not enter into the kingdom of heaven[384],' was Ignatius, who became patriarch of Antioch. He saw in a vision the angels ministering in two bands, and he ordained that (men) should minister in the church in like manner[385]. After some time this order was broken through; and when Diodorus went with his father on an embassy to the land of Persia, and saw that they ministered in two bands, he came to Antioch his country, and re-established the custom of their ministering in two bands[386].

The children whom they brought near to our Lord, that He might lay His hand upon them and pray, were Timothy and Titus, and they were deemed worthy of the office of bishop.

The names of the Maries who are mentioned in the Gospels. Mary the Virgin, the mother of our Lord; Mary the wife of Joseph; Mary the mother of Cleopas and Joseph; Mary the wife of Peter, the mother of Mark the Evangelist; and Mary the sister of Lazarus. Some say that Mary the sinner is Mary of Magdala; but others do not agree with this, and say that she was other than the Magdalene. Those who say that she was the Magdalene tell us that she built herself a tower with the wages of fornication; and those who say that she was other than the Magdalene, say that Mary Magdalene was called after the name of her town Magdala, and that she was a pure and holy woman.

THE NAMES OF THE EASTERN CATHOLICS, THE SUCCESSORS OF THE APOSTLES ADDAI AND MÂRÎ[387]

1. Addai was buried in Edessa.

2. Mârî (was buried) in the convent of Kônî[388].

3. Abrîs, called in Greek A[m]brosius; the place of his grave is unknown; he was of the laying on of hands of Antioch.

4. Abraham was of the laying on of hands of Antioch; he was descended from the family of Jacob the son of Joseph; his grave is in Ctesiphon.

5. James, of the laying on of hands of Antioch, was also of the family of Joseph the husband of Mary; his grave is in Ctesiphon.

6. Ahâ-d´abû[hî] was of the laying on of hands of Antioch; his grave is in Ctesiphon.

7. Shahlûphâ was of the laying on of hands of Ctesiphon, and he was buried there.

8. Pâpâ; his grave is at Ctesiphon.

9. Simon bar Sabbâ`ê was martyred at Shôshân.

10. Shah-dôst was buried in Ctesiphon.

11. Bar-Be`esh-shemîn[389] was martyred and buried in Elam (Khûzistân).

12. Tûmarsâ was buried in Ctesiphon.

13. Kâyômâ was buried in Ctesiphon; he abdicated the patriarchate, and another was put in his place, and was before him until he died.

14. Isaac was buried in Ctesiphon.

15. Ahâ was buried in Ctesiphon.

16. Yab-alâhâ was of the school of Mâr `Abdâ[390]; he was buried in Ctesiphon.

17. Ma`nâ dwelt in Persia and was buried there.

18. Dâd-îshô` was buried in Hêrtâ[391]. In his days the strife between Nestorius and Cyril (of Alexandria) took place.

19. Bâbôi was martyred and buried in Hêrtâ.

20. Akak (Acacius) was of the family of Bâbôi the Catholicus; he was buried in al-Madâïn[392].

21. Bâbai took a wife, and was buried at Ctesiphon,

22. Shîlâ took a wife, and was buried in his convent beside Awânâ[393].

23. Paul was buried in Ctesiphon.

24. Mâr(î)-abâ was buried in Hêrtâ, and was a martyr without bloodshed.

25. Ezekiel was buried in Hêrtâ.

26. Îshô`-yab of Arzôn[394] was buried in Hêrtâ.

27. Sabr-îshô` was buried in Hêrtâ.

28. Gregory was buried in . . . . . .

29. Îshô`-yab of Gedâlâ[395] was buried in . . . . . .

30. Mâr[î]-emmêh was buried in Ketîmiyâ (?).

31. Îshô`-yab of Adiabene[396] was buried in Bêth-`Âbê[397].

32. George was buried in . . . . . .

33. John was buried in . . . . . .

34. Henân-îshô` was buried in . . . . . .

35. Selîbâ-zekhâ was buried in Ctesiphon.

36. Pethiôn was buried in Ctesiphon.

37. Mâr[î]-abâ was buried in al-Madâïn.

38. Jacob was buried in . . . . . .

39. Henân-îshô` was buried in . . . . . .

40. Timothy was buried in his own convent.

41. Îshô` (Joshua) the son of Nôn (Nun) was buried in the convent of Timothy.

42. George was buried in the same convent.

43. Sabr-îshô`[398] was buried in the same convent.

44. Abraham was buried in the same convent.

45. Athanasius[399] was buried in the same convent.

46. Sergius was buried in the same convent.

47. Anôsh (Enos) was buried in the same convent.

48. John the son of Narsai was buried in the Greek Palace (at Baghdâd)[400].

49. Joannes[401] was buried in the Greek Palace.

50. John was buried in the Greek Palace.

51. Abraham was buried in the convent of `Abdôn.

52. Emmanuel was buried in the Greek Palace.

53. Israel was buried in the Greek Palace.

54. `Abd-îshô` was buried in the Greek Palace.

55. Mârî was buried in the Greek Palace.

56. Joannes[402] was buried in the Greek Palace.

57. John was buried in the Greek Palace.

58. Îshô`-yab was buried in the Grek Palace.

59. Elijah (Elîyâ) was buried in the Greek Palace.

60. John was buried in the Greek Palace.

61. Sabr-îshô` was buried in the Greek Palace.

62. `Abd-îshô` was buried in the Greek Palace.

63. Makkîkhâ was buried in the Greek Palace.

64. Elijah (Elîyâ) was buried in the Greek Palace.

65. Bar-saumâ was buried in the Greek Palace.

66. `Abd-îshô` was buried . . . . . .

67. Îshô`-yab was buried in the church of Mâr Sabr-îshô`.

68. Elijah (Elîyâ) was buried in the church of Mâr Sabr-îshô`.

69. Yab-alâhâ was buried in the church of Mârt[î] Maryam (my lady Mary).

70. Sabr-îshô` was buried in the church of Mârt[î] Maryam[403].

71. Sabr-îshô` was buried[404] . . . . . .

72. [Mâr Makkîkhâ was buried . . . . . .

73. Mâr Denhâ was buried . . . . . .

74. Mâr Yab-alâhâ the Turk[405] was buried . . . . . .

75. Mâr Timothy was buried . . . . . .

76. Mâr Denhâ was buried . . . . . .

77. Mâr Simon was buried . . . . . .

78. Mâr Elijah (Elîyâ) was buried . . . . . .

79. Mâr Simon of our days, may he live for ever![406]]

The names of the Catholics who were deposed and dismissed (from office): Mâr(î)-bôkht, Narsai, Elisha, Joseph and Sôrên.

THE NAMES OF THE KINGS WHO HAVE REIGNED IN THE WORLD FROM THE FLOOD UNTIL NOW

THE MEDIAN KINGS WHO REIGNED IN BABYLON

Darius the son of Vashtasp (Hystaspes) reigned 24 years.

Ahshîresh (Xerxes) his son, 20 years.

Artahshisht the long-hand (Artaxerxes Longimanus), 41 years.

Daryâwash (Darius) the son of the concubine, 20 years.

Artahshisht (Artaxerxes) the ruler, 30 years.

Arses the son of Ochus, 4 years.

Daryâwash (Darius) the son of Ârsham (Arsanes), 6 years.

THE YEARS OF THE EGYPTIAN KINGS[407]

Alexander the son of Philip, 12 years. Ptolemy the son of Lagôs, 40 years. Ptolemy Philadelphus, 38 years[408]. In his third year[409] the fifth millennium ended. This (king) asked the captive Jews who were in Egypt, and seventy old men translated the Scriptures for him, from Hebrew into Greek, in the island of Pharos. In return for this he set them free, and gave back to them also the vessels of their temple. Their names are these. Josephus, Hezekiah, Zechariah, John, Ezekiel, Elisha; these were of the tribe of Reuben. Judah, Simon, Samuel, Addai, Mattathias, Shalmî; these were of the tribe of Simeon. Nehemiah, Joseph, Theodosius, Bâsâ, Adonijah, Dâkî[410]; these were of the tribe of Levi. Jothan[411], Abdî, Elisha, Ananias, Zechariah, Hilkiah; these were of the tribe of Judah. Isaac, Jacob, Jesus, Sambât (Sabbateus), Simon, Levi; these were of the tribe of Issachar. Judah, Joseph, Simon, Zechariah, Samuel, Shamlî[412]; these were of the tribe of Zebulon. Sambât (Sabbateus), Zedekiah, Jacob, Isaac, Jesse, Matthias; these were of the tribe of Gad. Theodosius, Jason, Joshua, John, Theodotus, Jothan[413]; these were of the tribe of Asher. Abraham, Theophilus, Arsam, Jason, Jeremiah, Daniel; these were of the tribe of Dan. Jeremiah, Eliezer, Zechariah, Benaiah, Elisha, Dathî; these were of the tribe of Naphtali. Samuel, Josephus, Judah, Jonathan, Dositheus, Caleb; these were of the tribe of Joseph. Isalus, John, Theodosius, Arsam, Abijah[414], Ezekiel; these were of the tribe of Benjamin.

After Ptolemy Philadelphus arose Ptolemy Euergetes; (he reigned) 26 years[415].

Ptolemy Philopator, 17 years.

Ptolemy Epiphanes, 24 years.

Ptolemy Philometor, 35 years. The time of the Maccabees extended to this (reign), and in it the old Covenant came to an end.

Ptolemy Soter, 17 years[416].

Ptolemy Alexander, 18 years[417].

Ptolemy Dionysius, 30 years[418].

THE YEARS OF THE ROMAN EMPERORS

Gaius Julius, 4 years.

Augustus, 57 years. In the forty-third year of his reign our Lord Christ was born[419].

Tiberius, 23 years. In the fifteenth year of his reign our Lord was baptised; and in the seventeenth year He suffered, died, rose again, and ascended to heaven[420].

Gaius (Caligula), 4 years.

Claudius, 14 years.

Nero, 14 years.

Vespasian, 10 years. Immediately after he came to the throne, he sent his son Titus against Jerusalem, and he besieged it for two years, until he uprooted it and destroyed it.

Titus, 2 years.

Domitian, 15 years.

Trajan, 20 years[421]. John, the son of Zebedee, lived until the seventh year of his reign.

Hadrian, 20 years.

Antoninus, 20 years[422].

Verus, 20 years[423].

Commodus, 14 years[424].

Severus, 20 years[425].

The house of Antoninus.

Alexander the son of Mammaea, 13 years.

Maximinius and Gordianus, 9 years.

Philip and Gallus, 10 years.

Valerianus and Gallius (Gallienus), 15 years[426].

Claudius and Tacitus, 16 years[427].

Diocletian and those that were with him, 20 years.

Constantine, 33 years[428].

THE KINGS OF THE PERSIANS FROM SHÂBÔR (SAPOR) THE SON OF HORMIZD[429]

In the fourth year of Constantine Caesar the Victorious, Shâbôr reigned in Persia 70 years.

Ardashîr his brother, 20 years.

Vahrân (Bahrâm) and Shâbôr, the sons of Ardashîr, 20 years.

Yazdagerd, the son of Shâbôr, 20 years.

Vahrân (Bahrâm), the son of Yazdagerd, 20 years.

Pêrôz, the son of Yazdagerd, 27 years.

Balâsh, the son of Pêrôz, 4 years.

Kawâd, the son of Pêrôz, 41 years.

Chosrau, the son of Kawâd, 47 years.

Hormizd, the son of Chosrau, 12 years.

From Shâbôr to this fifteenth year of Chosrau the son of Hormizd, in which he destroyed Dârâ[430], is three hundred and six years. The sum of all the years from Adam to this fifteenth year of Chosrau the conqueror, which is the nine hundred and sixteenth year of the Greeks[431], is 5861 years. From Adam to the Crucifixion is 5280 years. The whole of the Jewish economy therefore, from the time they went out of Egypt until Jerusalem was destroyed by Titus, was 1601 years. From Abraham to this year is 2031 years.

OF THE YEARS THAT HAVE PASSED AWAY FROM THE WORLD

From Adam to the Flood was 2262 years. From the Flood to Abraham was 1015 years. From Abraham to the Exodus of the people from Egypt was 430 years. From the Exodus of the people by the hand of Moses to Solomon and the building of the Temple was 400 years. From Solomon to the first Captivity, which Nebuchadnezzar led away captive, was 495 years. From the first Captivity to the prophesying of Daniel was 180 years. From the prophesying of Daniel to the Birth of our Lord was 483 years. All these years make 5345 years[432]. From Alexander to our Lord was 303 years. From our Lord to Constantine was 341 years. In the year 438 of Alexander the Macedonian, the kingdom of the Persians had its beginning[433]. Know, O my brother readers, that from the beginning of the creation of Adam to Alexander was 5180 years.

OF THE END OF TIMES AND THE CHANGE OF KINGDOMS[434]; FROM THE BOOK OF METHODIUS, BISHOP OF ROME[435]

IN this seventh and last millennium will the kingdom of the Persians be destroyed. In it will the children of Ishmael go forth from the wilderness of Yathrib (al-Medînah), and they will all come and be gathered together in Gibeah of Ramah, and there shall the fat ones of the kingdom of the Greeks, who destroyed the kingdoms of the Hebrews and the Persians, be destroyed by Ishmael, the wild ass of the desert; for in wrath shall he be sent against the whole earth, against man and beast and trees, and it shall be a merciless chastisement. It is not because God loves them that He has allowed them to enter into the kingdoms of the Christians, but by reason of the iniquity and sin which is wrought by the Christians, the like of which has never been wrought in any one of the former generations. They are mad with drunkenness and anger and shameless lasciviousness; they have intercourse with one another wickedly, a man and his son committing fornication with one woman, the brother with his brother's wife, male with male, and female with female, contrary to the law of nature and of Scripture, as the blessed Paul has said, 'Male with male did work shame, and likewise also the women did work lewdness, and, contrary to nature, had intercourse with one another[436].' Therefore they have brought upon themselves the recompense of punishment which is meet for their error, women as well as men, and hence God will deliver them over to the impurity of the barbarians, that their wives may be polluted by the sons of pollution, and men may be subjected to the yoke of tribute; then shall men sell everything that they have and give it to them, but shall not be able to pay the debt of the tribute, until they give also their children to them into slavery. And the tyrant shall exalt himself until he demands tribute and poll-tax from the dead that lie in the dust, first oppressing the orphans and defrauding the widows. They will have no pity upon the poor, nor will they spare the miserable; they will not relieve the afflicted; they will smite the grey hairs of the aged, despise the wise, and honour fools; they will mock at those who frame laws, and the little shall be esteemed as the great, and the despised as the honourable; their words shall cut like swords, and there is none who shall be able to change the persuasive force of their words. The path of their chastisement shall be from sea to sea, and from east to west, and from north to south, and to the wilderness of Yathrib. In their latter days there shall be great tribulation, old men and old women hungering and thirsting, and tortured in bonds until they account the dead happy. They will rip up the pregnant woman, and tear infants away from their mothers' bosoms and sell them like beasts, and those that are of no use to them will they dash against the stones. They will slay the priests and deacons in the sanctuary, and they will lie with their wives in the houses of God. They will make clothes for themselves and their wives out of the holy vestments, and they will spread them upon their horses, and work impurity upon them in their beds. They will bring their cattle into the churches and altars, and they will tie up their dogs by the shrines of the saints. In those days the spirit of the righteous and of them that are well versed in signs will be grieved. The feeble will deny the true faith, the holy Cross, and the life-giving mysteries; and without compulsion many will deny Christ, and become rebels and slanderers and boasters, denying the faith. With this chastisement shall the Christians be tried. For at that time the righteous, the humble, the peaceful and the gentle will not be sought after, but liars and slanderers and accusers and disturbers and the obscene and those who are destitute of mercy, and those who scoff at their parents and blaspheme the life-giving mysteries. And the true believers shall come into troubles and persecutions until they despair of their lives. Honour shall be taken away from the priests, and the pastors shall become as the people. When the measure of their (i.e. the Ishmaelites') victory is full, tribulation will increase, and chastisement will be doubled upon man and beast. And there shall be a great famine, and the dead bodies of men shall lie in the streets and squares without any one to bury them, and (just) reckoning shall vanish and disappear from the earth, And men shall sell their brass and their iron and their clothes, and shall give their sons and their daughters willingly to the heathen. A man shall lie down in the evening and rise in the morning, and shall find at his do or two or three exactors and officers to carry off by force; and two or three women shall throw themselves upon one man and say, 'We will eat our own bread, and wear our own apparel, only let us take refuge beneath thy skirts[437].' When men are oppressed and beaten, and hunger and thirst, and are tormented by that bitter chastisement; while the tyrants shall live luxuriously and enjoy themselves, and eat and drink, and boast in the victory they have won, having destroyed nations and peoples, and shall adorn themselves like brides, saying, 'The Christians have neither a God nor a deliverer;' then all of a sudden there shall be raised up against them pains like those of a woman in childbirth; and the king of the Greeks shall go forth against them in great wrath, and he shall rouse himself like a man who has shaken off his wine. He shall go forth against them from the sea of the Cushites, and shall cast the sword and destruction into the wilderness of Yathrib and into the dwelling-place of their fathers. They shall carry off captive their wives and sons and daughters into the service of slavery, and fear of all those round about them shall fall upon them, and they shall all be delivered into the hand of the king of the Greeks, and shall be given over to the sword and to captivity and to slaughter, and their latter subjection shall be one hundred times more severe than their (former) yoke. They shall be in sore tribulation from hunger and thirst and anxiety; they shall be slaves unto those who served them, and bitter shall their slavery be. Then shall the earth which has become desolate of its inhabitants find peace, and the remnant that is left shall return every man to his own land and to the inheritance of his fathers; and men shall increase like locusts upon the earth which was laid waste. Egypt shall be ravaged, Arabia shall be burnt with fire, the land of Hebron shall be laid waste, and the tongue of the sea shall be at peace. All the wrath and anger of the king of the Greeks shall have full course upon those who have denied Christ. And there shall be great peace on earth, the like of which has not been from the creation of the world until its end; for it is the last peace. And there shall be great joy on earth, and men shall dwell in peace and quiet; convents and churches shall be restored, cities shall be built, the priests shall be freed from taxes, and men shall rest from labour and anxiety of heart. They shall eat and drink; there shall be neither pain nor care; and they shall marry wives and beget children during that true peace. Then shall the gates of the north be opened, and the nations shall go forth that were imprisoned there by Alexander the king.

OF GOG AND MAGOG, WHO ARE IMPRISONED IN THE NORTH

WHEN Alexander was king and had subdued countries and cities, and had arrived in the East, he saw on the confines of the East those men who are of the children of Japhet. They were more wicked and unclean than all (other) dwellers in the world; filthy peoples of hideous appearance, who ate mice and the creeping things of the earth and snakes and scorpions. They never buried the bodies of their dead, and they ate as dainties the children which women aborted and the after-birth. People ignorant of God, and unacquainted with the power of reason, but who lived in this world without understanding like ravening beasts. When Alexander saw their wickedness, he called God to his aid, and he gathered together and brought them and their wives and children, and made them go in, and shut them up within the confines of the North. This is the gate of the world on the north, and there is no other entrance or exit from the confines of the world from the east to the north. And Alexander prayed to God with tears, and God heard his prayer and commanded those two lofty mountains which are called 'the children of the north,' and they drew nigh to one another until there remained between them about twelve cubits. Then he built in front of them a strong building, and be made for it a door of brass, and anointed it within and without with oil of Thesnaktîs, so that if they should bring iron (implements) near it to force it open, they would be unable to move it; and if they wished to melt it with fire, it would quench it; and it feared neither the operations of devils nor of sorcerers, and was not to be overcome (by them). Now there were twenty-two kingdoms imprisoned within the northern gate, and tbeir names are these: Gôg, Mâgôg, Nâwâl, Eshkenâz[438], Denâphâr[439], Paktâyê, Welôtâyê[440], Humnâyê, Parzâyê, Daklâyê, Thaubelâyê[441], Darmetâyê, Kawkebâyê, Dog-men (Cynocephali), Emderâthâ, Garmîdô`, Cannibals[442], Therkâyê, Âlânâyê, Pîsîlôn, Denkâyê[443], Saltrâyê[444]. At the end of the world and at the final consummation, when men are eating and drinking and marrying wives, and women are given to husbands; when they are planting vineyards and building buildings, and there is neither wicked man nor adversary, on account of the assured tranquillity and certain peace; suddenly the gates of the north shall be opened and the hosts of the nations that are imprisoned there shall go forth. The whole earth shall tremble before them, and men shall flee and take refuge in the mountains and in caves and in burial places and in clefts of the earth; and they shall die of hunger; and there will be none to bury them, by reason of the multitude of afflictions which they will make men suffer. They will eat the flesh of men and drink the blood of animals; they will devour the creeping things of the earth, and hunt for serpents and scorpions and reptiles that shoot out venom, and eat them. They will eat dead dogs and cats[445], and the abortions of women with the after-birth; they will give mothers the bodies of their children to cook, and they will eat them before them without shame. They will destroy the earth, and there will be none able to stand before them. After one week of that sore affliction, they will all be destroyed in the plain of Joppa, for thither will all those (people) be gathered together, with their wives and their sons and their daughters; and by the command of God one of the hosts of the angels will descend and will destroy them in one moment.

OF THE COMING OF THE ANTICHRIST, THE SON OF PERDITION

IN a week and half a week[446] after the destruction of these wretches shall the son of destruction appear. He shall be conceived in Chorazin, born in Bethsaida, and reared in Capernaum. Chorazin shall exult because he was conceived in her, Bethsaida because he was born in her, and Capernaum because he was brought up in her; for this reason our Lord proclaimed Woe to these three (cities) in the Gospel[447]. As soon as the son of perdition is revealed, the king of the Greeks will go up and stand upon Golgotha, where our Lord was crucified; and he will set the royal crown upon the top of the holy Cross, upon which our Lord was crucified; and he will stretch out his two hands to heaven; and will deliver over the kingdom to God the Father. The holy Cross will be taken up to heaven, and the royal crown with it; and the king will die immediately. The king who shall deliver over the kingdom to God will be descended from the seed of Kûshath the daughter of Pîl, the king of the Ethiopians; for Armelaus (Romulus) the king of the Greeks took Kûshath to wife, and the seed of the Ethiopians was mingled with that of the Greeks. From this seed shall a king arise who shall deliver the kingdom over to God, as the blessed David has said, 'Cush will deliver the power to God[448].' When the Cross is raised up to heaven, straightway shall every head and every ruler and all powers be brought to nought, and God will withdraw His providential care from the earth. The heavens will be prevented from letting fall rain, and the earth from producing germs and plants; and the earth shall remain like iron through drought, and the heavens like brass. Then will the son of perdition appear, of the seed and of the tribe of Dan; and he will shew deluding phantasms, and lead astray the world, for the simple will see the lepers cleansed, the blind with their eyes opened, the paralytic walking, the devils cast out, the sun when he looks upon it becoming black, the moon when he commands it becoming changed, the trees putting forth fruit from their branches, and the earth making roots to grow. He will shew deluding phantasms (of this kind), but he will not be able to raise the dead. He will go into Jerusalem and will sit upon a throne in the temple saying, 'I am the Christ;' and he will be borne aloft by legions of devils like a king and a lawgiver, naming himself God, and saying, 'I am the fulfilment of the types and the parables.' He will put an end to prayers and offerings, as if at his appearance prayers are to be abolished and men will not need sacrifices and offerings along with him. He becomes a man incarnate by a married woman of the tribe of Dan. When this son of destruction becomes a man, he will be made a dwelling-place for devils, and all Satanic workings will be perfected in him. There will be gathered together with him all the devils and all the hosts of the Indians; and before all the Indians and before all men will the mad Jewish nation believe in him, saying, 'This is the Christ, the expectation of the world.' The time of the error of the Antichrist will last two years and a half, but others say three years and six months. And when every one is standing in despair, then will Elijah (Elias) come from Paradise, and convict the deceiver, and turn the heart of the fathers to the children and the heart of the children to the fathers; and he will encourage and strengthen the hearts of the believers.

OF DEATH AND THE DEPARTURE OF THE SOUL FROM THE BODY

THE foundation of all good and precious things, of all the greatness of God's gifts, of His true love, and of our arriving in His presence, is Death. Men die in five ways. Naturally; as David said, 'Unless his day come and he die,' alluding to Saul[449]. Voluntarily; as when Saul killed himself in the battle with the Philistines. By accident; such as a fall from a roof, and other fatal accidents. By violence, from devils and men and wild beasts and venomous reptiles. By (divine) chastisement; as the flood in the days of Noah, and the fire which fell upon the Sodomites, and other such like things. But (side by side) with all these kinds of fatalities runs the providence of God's government, which cannot be comprehended by the creatures, restraining (them) where it is meet (to restrain), and letting (them) loose where it is fitting (to let loose). This government is not comprehended in this world, neither by angels nor by men; but in the world which is to come all rational beings will know it. When the soul goes forth from the body, as Abbâ Isaiah says, the angels go with it: then the hosts of darkness go forth to meet it, seeking to seize it and examine it, if there be anything of theirs in it. Then the angels do not fight with them, but those deeds which the soul has wrought protect it and guard it, that they come not near it. If its deeds be victorious, then the angels sing praises before it until it meets God with joy. In that hour the soul forgets every deed of this world. Consequently, no one who does not obtain remission (of sins) in this world can be free from the penalty of examina-tion in that day. Not that there is torture or pleasure or recompense before the resurrection; but the soul knows everything that it has done whether of good or evil.

As to where the souls abide from the time they leave their bodies until the resurrection, some say that they are taken up to heaven, that is, to the region of spirit, where the celestial hosts dwell. Others say that they go to Paradise, that is, to the place which is abundantly supplied with the good things of the mystery of the revelations of God; and that the souls of sinners lie in darkness in the abyss of Eden outside Paradise. Others say that they are buried with their bodies; that is to say, as the two were buried in God at baptism, so also will they now dwell in Him until the day of the resurrection. Others say that they stand at the mouth of the graves and await their Redeemer; that is to say, they possess the knowledge of the resurrection of their bodies. Others say that they are as it were in a slumber, because of the shortness of the time; for they point out in regard to them that what seems to us a very long time is to them as a momentary nod (or wink) in its shortness[450]. And just as he that is sunk in slumber departs from the life of this world, and yet does not arrive at absolute mortality, so also are they in an intermediate knowledge which is higher than that of this world, and yet attain not to that which is after the resurrection. Those who say that they are like an infant which has no knowledge, shew that they call even the knowledge of the truth ignorance in comparison with that knowledge of the truth which shall be bestowed upon them after the resurrection.

That the souls of the righteous pray, and that their prayers assist those who take refuge with them, may be learned from many, especially from Mâr Theodore in his account of the blessed Thecla. Therefore it is right for those who have a holy man for a friend, to rejoice when he goes to our Lord in Paradise, because their friend has the power to help them by his prayers. Like the blind disciple of one of the saints mentioned in the Book of the Paradise, who, when his master was dying, wept bitterly and said, 'To whose care dost thou leave the poor blind man?' And his master encouraged him, and said to him, 'I believe in God that, if I find mercy in His sight, at the end of a week thou wilt see;' and after some days he did see. The souls of the righteous also hold spiritual conversation with each other, according to the Divine permission and command which moves them to this by necessary causes. Neither those who have departed this life in the flesh are hindered from this (intercourse), nor those who are still clad in their fleshly garments, if they live their life in them holily.

OF THE QUICKENING AND THE GENERAL RESUR-RECTION, THE CONSUMMATION OF THE MATERIAL WORLD AND THE BEGINNING OF THE NEW WORLD

AFTER Elijah comes and conquers the son of destruction, and encourages the believers, for a space and a time which is known to God alone, there will appear the living sign of our Lord's Cross, honoured and borne aloft in the hands of the Archangel Gabriel. Its light will overpower the light of the sun, to the reproach and putting to shame of the infidels and the crucifying Jews. As soon as the life-giving Cross appears before our Lord, as the Doctor saith, 'His victory comes before Him,' etc., then a powerful light will fill the whole vaulted space between the heavens and the earth, the radiance and light whereof will be above all (other) lights; and suddenly will the mighty sound of the first trumpet of the Archangel be heard, concerning which our Lord said, 'At midnight there will be a cry, "Behold the Bridegroom cometh, go ye forth to meet Him[451]."' At this trumpet the sun shall become dark, the moon shall not display its light, the stars shall drop from the heavens like leaves, and the powers of the heavens shall be moved. The earth shall totter and tremble, the mountains and hills shall melt, the sea shall be disturbed and shall cause terrible sounds to be heard. The rivers shall submerge the earth, the trees shall be uprooted, buildings shall fall, towns and villages shall be overturned, and high walls and strong towers shall be thrown down. The wild beasts and cattle and fowl and fish shall come to an end and perish; and everything shall be destroyed, except a few human beings who shall remain alive, and whom the resurrection shall overtake, of whom Paul has said, 'We who are left shall not overtake them that sleep[452],' meaning to say that those who are found alive at the time of the resurrection will not sleep the sleep of death; as the apostle says again, 'Behold I tell you a mystery; we shall not all sleep, but we shall all be changed[453].' As touching the heavens, some say that they will be rent, and that the waters which are above the firmament will descend, for it is not possible for the substance of water to pass through the substance of the firmament. Others say that as water passes through a tree or a piece of pottery, and sweat through the skin, so also will men enter into heaven and not be prevented, and (in like manner too) will the waters descend from above. Others say that the firmament will be rolled up like the curtain of a tent.

The second trumpet is that at the sound of which the firmament will be opened, and our Lord will appear from heaven in splendour and great glory. He will come down with the glory of His divinity as far as two-thirds of the distance between the firmament and the earth, whither Paul ascended in the spirit of revelation[454]. He will then make an end of the son of perdition, and destroy him body and soul, and He will hurl Satan and the devils into Gehenna.

The third trumpet is the last, at which the dead will rise, and the living be changed, as the blessed Paul says, 'Swiftly, as in the twinkling of an eye, at the last trumpet when it sounds; and the dead shall rise without corruption, and we shall be changed[455].' So swiftly and speedily will the resurrection of all men be wrought, according to the spiritual nature of the new world. For the swiftness of the resurrection will surpass the swiftness of understanding, and the spiritual hosts alone see and know in what manner it will take place, every man being suddenly found standing in his spirituality. Some men therefore have a tradition that the resurrection of the righteous and the just and the believers will precede that of other men, who are remote from the true faith; but according to the opinion of the truthful and of people generally, the resurrection of the whole human race will take place quicker than lightning and than the twinkling of an eye; from the generation of Adam to the latest generation they shall rise at the last trumpet. And though, according to the opinion of the Expositor[456], many sounds will be heard on that night, each one of which is a sign of what will happen, yet, according to the consent of the greater part of the expositors and of Scripture, three distinct trumpets will sound by which the whole work of the resurrection will be completed and finished. Michael the expositor and exegete, however, says otherwise in the book of Questions[457], speaking as follows: 'The world will not pass away and be dissolved before the vivification of the dead, but the coming of our Lord will be seen first of all, who will come with the spiritual hosts; and immediately our Lord's power will compel the earth to give up the parts of the bodies of men who have been slain and have become dust and ashes within it; and there will be a making ready and preparation of the souls to receive their bodies all together. If, before the vivification of the dead, the world and all that is therein were to pass away, from whence pray would the dead rise? Those who say that the world will pass away before the vivification of the dead are fools and simpletons; for Christ will not make the world pass away before the vivification of the dead, but He will first of all raise the dead, and men will see with their eyes the passing away of the world, the uprooting of the elements, and the destruction of the heavens and the earth and the sun and the moon and the stars; and from here sorrow will begin to reign in the mind of the wicked, and endless joy in the mind of the righteous.

OF THE MANNER AND STATE IN WHICH MEN WILL RISE IN THE DAY OF THE RESURRECTION

ALL classes and conditions of men will rise from the dead in the state of the perfect form of Christ, about thirty-three years of age, even as our Redeemer rose from the grave. We shall rise with all our limbs perfect, and with the same constitutions, without addition or diminution. Some say that the hair and nails and prepuce will rise, and some say they will not; as if they were superfluous for the completion of the nature of man. Some say concerning the resurrection that a likeness only will rise, without parts and without the composition of the limbs of man; a mere similitude of hands and feet and hardness of bones. Others say that the whole man will be cast into one crystalline substance, and that all his parts will be mingled together; and they do not grant him an ordered arrangement of composition. Others say that the vessels which are inside the belly, such as the bowels, liver, etc., will not rise; but they err and stray from the truth, and do not understand that if one of the parts of the body perish, it is not perfect. For Paul shewed plainly and laid down an example of the resurrection in the grain of wheat: just as that grows up entire with its glory, without any portion of it having perished, even so we; for the whole man shall rise with all his limbs and parts, and ordered in his composition as now, only having acquired purification from the humours. And this is not surprising, that if an earthen vessel acquires firmness and lightness when it goes into the fiery furnace, without any change taking place in its shape or form, but is lightened of its heaviness and density, whilst it preserves its shape uninjured; so also should the Holy Spirit burn us in the furnace of the resurrection and drive forth from us all the foul material of the present (life), and clothe us with incorruptibility. 'It is sown an animal body; it rises a spiritual body[458].' We shall neither see nor hear with all our bodily members, although some men have thought that the whole man will be sight and hearing; but we shall carry out action with these same usual limbs, if it happen to be necessary; although we shall not there need speech and conversation with one another, because each other's secrets will be revealed to us.

The things which certain stupid men invent, who indulge their fancy, and give bodily form to the punishment of sinners and the reward of the just and righteous, and say that there is at the resurrection a reckoning and a pair of scales, the Church does not receive; but each one of us carries his light and his fire within him, and his heaviness and his lightness is round in his own pature. Just as stone and iron naturally possess the property of falling to the earth, and as the air naturally ascends upward on account of its rarity and its lightness; so also in the resurrection, he that is heavy and lying in sins, his sins will bring him down; and he that is free from the rust of sin, his purity will make him rise in the scale. And our Lord will ascend to heaven, and the angels (will go) before Him like ambassadors, and the just and the righteous will be upon His right hand and His left, and the children behind Him in the form of the life-giving Cross.

OF THE HAPPINESS OF THE RIGHTEOUS AND THE TORMENT OF SINNERS, AND IN WHAT STATE THEY ARE THERE

IT is right for us to know and explain how those suffer, who suffer in Gehenna. If they do suffer, how can we say that they are impassible? and if they do not suffer, then there is no torture for sinners; and if there be no torture for sinners in proportion to their sins, neither can there be happiness for the righteous as a reward for their labours. The suffering wherewith the Fathers say that sinners will suffer in Gehenna is not one that will pain the limbs, such as the blows of sticks, the mutilation of the flesh, and the breaking of the bones, but one that will afflict the soul, such as grief for the transgression of what is right, repentance for shameful deeds, and banishment from one to whom he is bound in love and for whom his affection is strong. For in the resurrection we shall not be without perception, like the sun which perceives not his splendour, nor the moon her brilliancy, nor the pearl its beauty; but by the power of reason we shall feel perfectly the delight of our happiness or the keen pain of our torture. So then by that which enables the righteous to perceive the pleasure of their happiness, by that selfsame thing will the wicked also perceive the suffering of their torment; (that is) by the power capable of receiving pleasure, which is the intelligence. Hence it is right for us to be certain that intelligence will not be taken away from us, but it will receive the utmost purification and refinement. The glorious and good things of the world which is to come are not to be compared with those of this world; for if all the glorious and good things and delights of this world were given to us in the world which is to come, we should look upon them as hateful and abominable, and they would not be able to give us pleasure or to gladden us; and our nature by the blessedness of its immortality would be exalted above all their glory and desirability. And if all the torments and afflictions and troubles of this world were brought near to us in the world which is to come, the pain of them would make no impression upon our immortal and immutable nature. Hence the pleasure of that world is something beyond all comparison more glorious and excellent and exalted than those of this world; and the torment of yonder is likewise something beyond all comparison more severe and more bitter than any that is here.

It is also right for us to explain the quality of the light of the righteous. The light of the righteous is not of a natural origin like this elemental light (of ours), but some of the light of our Lord--whose splendour surpasses ten thousand suns--is diffused and shed upon them. Each saint shines in proportion to his purity, and holiness and refinement and sincerity, as the blessed Paul has said, 'One star surpasseth another in glory, so also is the resurrection of the dead[459].' And although all the saints will be happy in one kingdom, yet he who is near to the King or the Bridegroom will be separated from him whose place is at the end of the guest-chamber, even though his place be in the same chamber. So also with the sinners in Gehenna; their sentence will not be alike, for in proportion to the sin of each will be his torment. And as the light of the sun is not to be compared with the light of the moon, nor is the light of the moon like that of the stars, so also will the happiness of the righteous be, although the name and honour of righteousness be laid upon and spread over all of them. And as the light of our Lord's humanity will pass over all our limbs without distinction, and take the place of dress and ornament for us, so also with all our members shall we perceive the suffering and torment of Gehenna. The festal garments which our Lord has prepared for His saints, the children of light, are impassibility; and the filthy garments which hinder us from entering into the spiritual bridal-chamber are the passions. In the new world there will be no distinctive names for ranks and conditions of human beings; and as every name and surname attributed to God and the angels had its origin from this world, and names for human beings were assigned and distributed by the government of this world, in the world of spiritual and intellectual natures there will be neither names nor surnames among them, nor male nor female, nor slave nor free, nor child nor old man, nor Ethiopian nor Roman (Greek); but they will all rise in the one perfect form of a man thirty-three years of age, as our Lord rose from the dead. In the world to come there will be no companies or bands but two; the one of the angels and the righteous, who will mingle and form one Church, and the other of the devils and sinners in Gehenna.

WHETHER MERCY WILL BE SHEWN TO SINNERS AND THE DEVILS IN GEHENNA, AFTER THEY HAVE BEEN TORMENTED AND SUFFERED AND BEEN PUNISHED, OR NOT? AND IF MERCY IS TO BE SHEWN TO THEM, WHEN WILL IT BE

SOME of the Fathers terrify us beyond our strength and throw us into despair; and their opinion is well adapted to the simple-minded and trangressors of the law. Others of them encourage us and bid us rely upon Divine mercy; and their opinions are suitable and adapted to the perfect and those of settled minds and the pious. In the 'Book of Memorials' it is thus written: 'This world is the world of repentance, but the world which is to come is the world of retribution. As in this world repentance saves until the last breath, so in the world to come justice exacts to the uttermost farthing. And as it is impossible to see here strict justice unmingled with mercy, so it is impossible to find there strict justice mingled with mercy.' Mâr Isaac says thus: 'Those who are to be scourged in Gehenna will be tortured with stripes of love; they who feel that they have sinned against love will suffer harder and more severe pangs from love than the pain that springs from fear.' Again he says: 'The recompense of sinners will be this: the resurrection itself will be their recompense instead of the recompense of justice; and at the last He will clothe those bodies which have trodden down His laws with the glory of perfection. This act of grace to us after we have sinned is greater than that which, when we were not, brought our nature into being.' Again he says: 'In the world which is to come grace will be the judge and not justice.' Mâr Theodore the Expositor says: 'Those who have here chosen fair things will receive in the world to come the pleasure of good things with praises; but the wicked who have turned aside to evil things all their life, when they are become ordered in their minds by penalties and the fear that springs from them, and choose good things, and learn how much they have sinned by having persevered in evil things and not in good things, and by means of these things receive the knowledge of the highest doctrine of the fear of God, and become instructed to lay hold of it with a good will, will be deemed worthy of the happiness of the Divine liberality. For He would never have said, "Until thou payest the uttermost farthing," unless it had been possible for us to be freed from our sins through having atoned for them by paying the penalty; neither would He have said, "he shall be beaten with many stripes," or "he shall be beaten with few stripes," unless it were that the penalties, being meted out according to the sins, should finally come to an end.' These things the Expositor has handed down in his books clearly and distinctly.

So also the blessed Diodorus, who says in the 'Book of the Dispensation[460]:' 'A lasting reward, which is worthy of the justice of the Giver, is laid up for the good, in return for their labours; and torment for sinners, but not everlasting, that the immortality which is prepared for them may not be worthless. They must however be tormented for a short time, as they deserve, in proportion to the measure of their iniquity and wickedness, according to the amount of the wickedness of their deeds. This they will have to bear, that they suffer for a short time; but immortal and unending happiness is prepared for them. If it be then that the rewards of good deeds are as great (in proportion to them) as the times of the immortality which are prepared for them are longer than the times of the limited contests which take place in this world, the torments for many and great sins must be very much less than the greatness of mercy. So then it is not for the good only that the grace of the resurrection from the dead is intended, but also for the wicked; for the grace of God greatly honours the good, but chastises the wicked sparingly.'

Again he says: 'God pours out the wages of reward beyond the measure of the labours (wrought), and in the abundance of His goodness He lessens and diminishes the penalty of those who are to be tormented, and in His mercy He shortens and reduces the length of the time. But even thus He does not punish the whole time according to (the length of) the time of folly, seeing that He requites them far less than they deserve, just as He does the good beyond the measure and period (of their deserts); for the reward is everlasting. It has not been revealed whether the goodness of God wishes to punish without ceasing the blameworthy who have been found guilty of evil deeds (or not), as we have already said before.   *
*   *   *   *   *   *   *   *   *   *   *   *

*[461] But if punishment is to be weighed out according to sin, not even so would punishment be endless. For as regards that which is said in the Gospel, 'These shall go away into everlasting punishment, but the righteous into life eternal[462];' this word 'eternal' (le-`âlam) is not definite: for if it be not so, how did Peter say to our Lord, 'Thou shalt never wash my feet[463],' and yet He washed him? And of Babylon He said, 'No man shall dwell

therein for ever and ever[464],' and behold many generations dwell therein. In the 'Book of Memorials' he says: 'I hold what the most celebrated of the holy Fathers say, that He cuts off a little from much. The penalty of Gehenna is a man's mind; for the punishment there is of two kinds, that of the body and that of the mind. That of the body is perhaps in proportion to the degree of sin, and He lessens and diminishes its duration; but that of the mind is for ever, and the judgment is for ever.' But in the New Testament le-`âlam is not without end. To Him be glory and dominion and praise and exaltation and honour for ever and ever. Amen and Amen.

ENDNOTES

[1] The proper names of the Nestorians strongly resemble those of our Puritans: Jesus-is-risen; Our-Lord-hath-converted; Jesus-hath-answered-me; Blessed-be-His-will; etc. (p. 1)

[2] For a full account of the contents of this MS. see Wright's Apocryphal Acts of the Apostles, vol. i, p. x. (p. 1)

[3] {T}he last Sunday of the Week of the Apostles, i.e. the first Sunday of the New Year. The word is compounded of the Persian nau-sard, 'New Year,' and êl, 'God,' meaning 'the Church's-New Year.' See Rosen p. v and Forshall's Catal., pp. 31 and 50; Wright's Catal., vol. i, p. 185 a, no. 101; 190 a, no. 81; Nöldeke, Tabari, p. 407, note 3; Hoffmann, Auszüge aus syr. Akten pers. Märtyrer, p. 59, note 523; Payne Smith, Thes. Syr., col. 2326; Lagarde, Armen. Studien, p. 111, no. 1601. (p. 2)

[4] On Hômô of Alkôsh see Hoffmann, Opuscula Nestoriana, pp. i and xxiii. (p. 2)

[5] On Hôrdephnê or Hôrdephnî, called also Kolpein, see Badger's Nestorians and their Riluals, vol. i, p. 254; Wright, Catal. Syr. MSS., p. 1067 a; and Hoffmann, Auszüge aus syr. Akten pers. Märtyrer, p. 195, note 1544. (p. 2)

[6] I.e. Tytnâye, about one hour's ride north of Tel Kêf, north of Mosul. Batnâye contains two churches; one dedicated to Mâr Cyriacus, and the other to Mârt Maryam El-`adhrâ, i.e. the blessed virgin Mary. See E. Sachau, Reise in Syrien und Mesopotamien, Leipzig, 1883, p. 360. (p. 3)

[7] I have seen a MS. the fly-leaves of which are made of the same sort of paper, and with the same marks, which is certainly not more than sixty years old. (p. 3)

[8] See Catalogus codd. manuscriptorum Bibl. Reg. Monacensis. Tomi primi pars 4ta codd. Orientales praeter Hebraeos et Arabicos et Persicos complectens (Munich, 1875), p. 114, Cod. Syr. 7. Schoenfelder's mistake is not corrected here. (p. 3)

[9] See Payne Smith, Catalogi Codd. MSS. Bibl. Bodl. Pars sexta, coll. 452-458, and ff. 81 b-212 b of Poc. 79 = Uri Cod. Syr. lxxxi. (p. 3)

[10] See Zotenberg, Catalogues des MSS. Syr. el Sabéens (Mandaïtes) de la Bibl. Nat. (Paris, 1874), no. 232, 1°, page 177. This Kârshûni MS. is imperfect at the beginning and end, and also wants some chapters in the middle. (p. 4)

[11] Assemânî is mistaken in his remarks about this name both in the Bibl. Or., t. iii, pt. i, p. 310, note 4, and in the Vatican Catalogue, t. iii, p. 367. (p. 4)

[12] See Le Quien, Oriens Christianus, vol. ii. 1212. (p. 6)

[13] 2 Cor. xii. 14. (p. 6)

[14] See Le Quien, Or. Christ., vol. ii. 1188. (p. 6)

[15] Khônî-Shâbôr, or Bêth-Wâzîk, was a town on the little Zâb, close to its junction with the Tigris, in the diocese of Tîrhân. Bêth-Wâzîk is also written Bêth-Wâzîg, and has been altered by the Arabs into al-Bawâzîg or al-Bawâzîj. See Hoffmann, Auszüge aus syrischen Akten persischer Märtyrer, pp. 189 and 296. It has, of course, nothing whatever to do with Gundê-Shâbôr, or Jundai-Shâbûr, with which it has sometimes been confounded. (p. 6)

[16] 1 John iv. 18. (p. 7)

[17] ### Θεόφοροι {Greek: ðεóforoi}; see Prov. xxv. 16. Schoenfelder, quippe a Theodoro dictum est. (p. 7)

[18] Schoenfelder, satiaberis fortasse de eo et prophetabis. (p. 7)

[19] C reads: The names of the Eastern Catholics, the successors of the Apostles. (p. 9)

[20] Ps. xc. 1, 2. (p. 11)

[21] See Bezold, Die Schatzhöhle, p. 7; Brit. Mus. Add. 25,875, fol. 7 a, col. 2: 'At the third hour they entered Paradise, for three hours they enjoyed the good things, for three hours they were ashamed, and at the ninth hour their expulsion from Paradise took place.' (p. 11)

[22] Gen. ii. 7. (p. 11)

[23] 1 Cor. iii. 16. (p. 11)

[24] 2 Cor. vi. 16; Ex. xxix. 45; Lev. xxvi. 12. (p. 11)

[25] Gen. i. 2, a chaotic waste. (p. 13)

[26] Gen. i. 2. (p. 13)

[27] This view is maintained in the 'Cave of Treasures,' Brit. Mus. Add. 25,875, fol. 3 b, col. 1: 'And on the first day of the week the Holy Spirit, one of the Persons of the Trinity, brooded upon the waters: and through His brooding upon the face of the waters they were blessed that they might be bringers forth.' See Bezold's translation, Die Schatzhöhle, p. 1; and Schoenfelder's note 26, on p. 9 of his translation of The Bee. (p. 13)

[28] 1 Kings viii. 27. (p. 14)

[29] Ps. cxlviii. 4. (p. 14)

[30] 'Dionysium Areopagitam sequitur Bassorensis in hac materia. Sufficit nomen tantum Hierarchiae coelestis dixisse.' Schoenfelder, note 28, p. 10. (p. 15)

[31] Colossians i. 16, 'thrones, or dominions, or principalities, or powers.' (p. 15)

[32] 'Motion' or 'movement,' Zau`â. 'Angelus est substantia intellectualis semper mobilis.' Schoenfelder, note 29, p. 10. (p. 15)

[33] Rev. iv. 6, 8; Ezek. i. 18. (p. 15)

[34] Isaiah vi. 2. (p. 15)

[35] Heb. ix. 11. (p. 16)

[36] According to the 'Cave of Treasures,' these were created on the first day. See Bezold's translation, p. 1, and Brit. Mus. Add. 25,175, fol. 1 b, col. 1. {This is not the same MS. Budge translated in his own edition of the book.} (p. 16)

[37] Or Commentator, that is Theodore of Mopsuestia. See Assemani, Bibl. Orient., iii. 1. 30. (p. 16)

[38] Schoenfelder, similitudinem aetheris, qui etc. (p. 16)

[39] Heb. ix. 7. (p. 16)

[40] Gen. i. 3. (p. 19)

[41] Meaning, probably, Theodore of Mopsuestia. (p. 19)

[42] Solomon seems to refer to Job, chap. xxxviii. 7. (p. 19)

[43] Gen. i. 6. (p. 20)

[44] Gen. i. 9. (p. 21)

[45] Comp. Jer. v. 22. (p. 21)

[46] Gen. i. 12. (p. 21)

[47] According to Rabbi Eliezer, chap. iii (Horowitz, חרגא חורגא {Hebrew: AGhDhX AGhDhVX}, part i, Leipzig, 1881), Paradise was one of the seven things created before the world. (p. 21)

[48] Gen. i. 14. (p. 22)

[49] See Exod. xii. 18. (p. 22)

[50] Gen. i. 21. (p. 23)

[51] Gen. i. 25. (p. 24)

[52] Gen. i. 26. (p. 25)

[53] Among other things, Jewish tradition says that the first Adam had two faces; that he was formed in two parts, on the one side male, and on the other female; that in height he reached from earth to heaven (Chagîgâh, p. 12, col. 1); and that he could stretch from one end of the world to the other (Sêpher Hasîdîm, No. 500). (p. 25)

[54] Gen. ii. 7. (p. 25)

[55] See Bezold, Die Schatzhöhle, pp. 3 and 4; and Brit. Mus. Add. 25,875, fol. 4 b, col. 1, line 23 to fol. 5 b, col. 1, line 14: 'The creation of Adam was on this wise. On the sixth day, which is Friday, at the first hour, p. 17 when silence reigned over all the ranks of the (heavenly) hosts, God said, "Come, let us make man in our image after our likeness"--hereby making known concerning the glorious Persons (of the Trinity). When the angels heard these words they were in fear and trembling, saying one to another, "We shall see a great miracle to-day, the likeness of God our Maker." And they saw the right hand of God stretched out and extended over the whole world; and all created things were collected in the palm of His right hand. And they saw that He took a grain of dust from all the earth, a drop of water from the whole nature of water, a breath of wind from all the atmosphere above, and a little warmth from all the nature of fire. And the angels saw when these four feeble elements--that is, cold and heat and dryness and moisture--were laid in the palm of His right hand, and God formed Adam. For what reason did God make

Adam out of these four elements, unless it were that through them everything in the world should be subject unto him? He took a grain of dust, that all natures which are of dust might be subject unto Adam; and a drop of water, that all those in the seas and rivers might be his; and a breath of air, that all kinds of birds of the air might be given unto him; and the heat of fire, that all the fiery beings and (heavenly) hosts might come to his aid. And God formed man with His holy hands, in His image and likeness. When the angels saw his glorious appearance, they trembled at the beauty of his appearance; for they saw the form of his face blazing with glorious beauty like the sphere of the sun, and the light of his eyes was like the sun, and the form of his body like the light of crystal. And when he stretched himself, and stood in the centre of the earth, he set his two feet on the spot where the cross of our Redeemer was placed: for Adam was created in Jerusalem, and there it was that he put on royal apparel, and the crown of glory was set upon his head; and there was he made king and priest and prophet, there did God set him upon the throne of His glory; and there He made him master over all creatures. And all beasts and cattle and fowl were gathered together, and they passed before Adam and he gave them names; and they bowed their heads to him, and all natures did homage to him and were subject unto him. And the angels and (heavenly) hosts heard the voice of God saying to him, "Adam, behold I have made thee king and priest and prophet and lord and chief and governor of all things made and created; to thee shall they be subject, and thine shall they be: and I have given thee power over everything that I have created." And when the angels heard these words, they all blessed and worshipped him.' (p. 25)

[56] So also Bar Hebraeus in the Ausar Râzê or Horreum Mysteriorum, Brit. Mus. Add. 21,580, fol. 32 a, col. 1. (p. 25)

[57] Gen. ii. 18. (p. 26)

[58] So also Bar Hebraeus in the Ausar Râzê Brit. Mus. Add. 21,580, fol. 32 a, col. 1. (p. 26)

[59] According to Rabbi Joshua of Sichnîn, God did not form Eve from Adam's head, that she might not carry her head proudly; nor from his eye, that she might not be curious; nor from his ear, that she might not be an eavesdropper; nor from his mouth, that she might not be gossiping; nor from his heart, that she might not be quarrelsome; nor from his hand, that she might not touch everything with her hand; nor from his feet, that she might not rove about. Berêshîth Rabbâh on Gen. ii. 22. Wünsche, Der Midrash Ber. Rab., Leipzig, 1881, p. 78. On Sichnîn, see Neubaner, La Géographie du Talmud, p. 204. (p. 26)

[60] Gen. ii. 23. (p. 26)

[61] Gen. ii. 9-17. (p. 27)

[62] Or Bâ-Zabdâ, a district on the western or right bank of the Tigris, adjacent to Jazîrat Ibn ʻOmar. (p. 27)

[63] Add. 25,875, fol. 6 a, col. 1, and see Bezold, Die Schatzhöhle, p. 5. (p. 27)

[64] Gen. xxvi. 20. (p. 28)

[65] Gen. xxxi. 47. i (p. 28)

[66] 'The tree of Life pre-figured the Cross of the Saviour, and it was this that was fixed in the middle of the earth.' Bezold, Die Schatzhöhle, p. 5; Brit. Mus. Add. 25,875, fol. 6 b, col. 1. (p. 28)

[67] The Rabbis thought that it was either the date-palm, the vine, the ethrôg ('citron-tree'), or the fig-tree. Midrash Rabbâh on Gen. ii. 9, 10; Wünsche, p. 69. (p. 28)

[68] Gen. iii. 6-24. (p. 29)

[69] 'And he went and dwelt in the serpent, and carried him and made him fly through the air to the skirts of Paradise. Why did he enter into the serpent and hide himself (there)? Because he knew that his appearance was hideous, and that if Eve saw his form she would straightway flee from him. As one who teaches a bird* the Greek tongue, brings a large mirror and places it between himself and the bird, and then begins to speak to her; and the bird as soon as it hears his voice turns round, and seeing its own form in the mirror straightway rejoices, thinking that it is a companion speaking with her, and thus willingly inclines her ear and listens to the words of him that talks with her, and pays attention (to them) and learns to talk Greek; so also did Satan enter in and dwell in the serpent.' Bezold, Die Schatzhöhle, p. 6; Brit. Mus. Add. 25,875, fol. 6 b, col. 1. (p. 29)

[70] These garments were softer than the linen and silk worn by kings; Bezold, Die Schatzhöhle, p. 7; Brit. Mus. Add. 25,875, fol. 7 a, col. 2. (p. 31)

[71] See chap. xxx. (p. 31)

[72] The 'Cave of Treasures' relates the story of Cain's birth and the dispute of the brothers thus: 'When Adam wished to know Eve his wife, he took from the skirts of Paradise gold, myrrh, and frankincense, and put them in a cave: and he blessed it and sanctified it that it might be the house of prayer of himself and of his sons, and he called it the "Cave of Treasures." And Adam and Eve came down from that holy

mountain to its skirts below; and there Adam knew Eve his wife. Some say that Adam knew Eve thirty years after they had gone forth from Paradise. And she conceived and bare Cain and Lebôdâ his sister with him; and again she conceived and bare Abel and Kelêmath his sister with him. When the youths had grown up, Adam said to Eve, "Let Cain take to wife Kelêmath who was born with Abel, and let Abel take Lebôdâ who was born with Cain." But Cain said to Eve his mother, "I will take to wife my own sister, and let Abel take his;" for Lebôdâ was beautiful. When Adam heard these words, he was very grieved, and said, "It is a transgression of the law that thou shouldst take to wife thy sister who was born with thee. But take ye of the fruit of the trees and the young of the flocks, and go ye up to the top of this holy mountain, and enter into the Cave of Treasures, and offer up your offerings there, and pray before God, and then be united unto your wives." And it came to pass that when Adam the first priest, and Cain and Abel his sons, were going up to the top of the mountain, Satan suggested to Cain to slay Abel his brother for the sake of Lebôdâ, and because his offering was rejected and not accepted before God, while that of Abel was accepted. And Cain increased his envy against Abel his brother; and when they came down to the plain, Cain stood up against Abel his brother and slew him by a wound from a flint stone.' See Bezold, Die Schatzhöhle, p. 8; Brit. Mus. Add. 25,875, fol. 7 b, col. 2 to fol. 8 a, col. 2. (p. 32)

[73] According to R. Hûnâ, Cain wished to marry his sister because she was born with him, Berêshith Rabbâh on Gen. iv. 8. (p. 32)

[74] According to Gen. v. 3, in the one hundredth and thirtieth year. The Oxford MS. gives the 233rd year. (p. 32)

[75] Gen. vi. 2. (p. 32)

[76] 'And the sons of Seth had intercourse with the daughters of Cain; and they conceived by them and brought forth mighty men, the sons of heroes, like towers, Hence early writers have erred and written, "The angels came down from heaven, and had intercourse with mankind, and from them were born mighty men of renown," But this is not true; they have said this because they did not understand, Now see, my brother readers, and know that this is neither in the nature of spiritual beings, nor in the nature of the impure and evil-doing demons who love adultery; for there are no males nor females among them, nor has there been even one added to their number since they fell. If the devils were able to have intercourse with women, they would not leave one single virgin undefiled in the whole human race.' See Bezold, Die Schatzhöhle, p. 18; and Brit. Mus. Add. 25,875, fol. 14 b, col. 2. p. 28 'Seth became a leader to the children of his people, and he ruled them in purity and holiness. And because of their purity they received this name, which is better than all names, that they should be called the children of God . . . . and they went up in place of that band of demons which fell from

heaven, to praise and glorify on the skirts of Paradise.' See Bezold, Die Schatzhöhle, p. 10; and Brit. Mus. Add. 25,875, fol. 9 a, col. 2. (p. 32)

[77] 'Our father died at the 9th hour of Friday, the 14th of the month of Nîsân, 930 years after the creation of the world, and gave up his soul to his Maker at the same hour in which the Son of Man on the Cross gave up His soul to His Father.' See Bezold, Die Schatzhöhle, p. 9; Brit. Mus. Add. 25,875, fol. 9 a, col. 1. (p. 33)

[78] 105 years, Gen. v. 6. (p. 33)

[79] In the Oxford MS. 905 years. (p. 33)

[80] 90 years, Gen. v. 9. (p. 33)

[81] The Oxford MS. omits this passage. (p. 33)

[82] 70 years, Gen. v. 12. The Oxford MS. has 920 years. (p. 33)

[83] 65 years, Gen. v. 15. (p. 33)

[84] In the Oxford MS. 833 years. (p. 33)

[85] 65 years, Gen. v. 21. (p. 33)

[86] In the Oxford MS. 774 years. This MS. omits to say how old the patriarchs were when they begat their sons. (p. 33)

[87] Gen. iv. 22. (p. 34)

[88] This name seems to have crept into the text by mistake. See Gen. iv. 22. (p. 34)

[89] 'They put together and made all kinds of music: Jubal made flutes and cithers and pipes, and the devils entered into them and dwelt in them; and when they blew into them, the devils sang inside the flutes, and made a noise from within them. And Tubal-cain made cymbals and rattles and hand drums.' Bezold, Die Schatzhöhle, p. 14; Brit. Mus. Add. 25,875, fol. 12 a, col. 1. (p. 34)

[90] Bezold, Die Schatzhöhle, p. 11. (p. 34)

[91] See Gen. vi-viii. (p. 35)

[92] For a description of the manners of the people at the time of Tubal-cain, see Bezold, Die Schatzhöhle, pp. 14, 15; Brit. Mus. Add. 25,875, fol. 12. (p. 35)

[93] Gen. vi. 16. 'The lower one for the beasts and cattle, the middle for the feathered fowl, and in the upper shalt thou and the children of thy house be. And make in it reservoirs for water, and garners for food. And make thee a gong (nâkûs) of teak wood uneaten by worms; its height shall be three cubits, and its breadth one and a half; and a hammer of the same. Thou shaltst strike it three times a day: once in the morning that the workmen may be gathered together for the work of the ark, once in the middle of the day for their food, and once at sunset that they may leave off.' Bezold, Die Schatzhöhle, p. 17; Brit. Mus. Add. 25,875, fol. 14 a, col. 2. (p. 35)

[94] 'Set thou Adam's body in the middle of the ark . . . . . . Thou and thy sons shalt be in the eastern part of the ark, and thy wife and thy sons' wives shall be in the western part.' Bezold, Die Schatzhöhle, p. 19; Brit. Mus. Add. 25,875, fol. 15 b, col. 1. (p. 35)

[95] 'Noah went into the ark at eventide on Friday the 17th of the blessed month Îyâr.' Bezold, Die Schatzhöhle, p. 21; Brit. Mus. Add. 25,875, fol. 17 a, col. 1. (p. 35)

[96] 'The angel of the Lord stood upon the outside of the ark to act as pilot.' Bezold, Die Schatzhöhle, p. 23; Brit. Mus. Add. 25,875, fol. 17 b, col. 2. (p. 35)

[97] טררא ירה לע = ודרק ירוט לע, Targûm Onkelos, Gen. viii. 4, i.e. the Jabal al-Jûdi of the Arabs, on the left bank of the Tigris, over against Jazîrat Ibn `Omar. (p. 36)

[98] 'The tenth month is Kânûn, but I saw Shebât written in the copy which I copied.' This is evidently the gloss of a careful scribe, which has crept into the text. (p. 36)

[99] See Hoffmann, Auszüge aus syrzschen Akten persischer Märtyrer, p. 174. (p. 36)

[100] Sûbâ = Nisîbis, from a false identification of the latter with the biblical צוֹבָה {Hebrew: CÔBhâÂ}. (p. 36)

[101] 'Why, since the whole sin belonged to Ham, was Canaan cursed except that, when the boy grew up and came to years of discretion, Satan entered into him and became a teacher of sin to him? and he renewed the work of the house of Cain the murderer.' Bezold, Die Schatzhöhle, p. 25; Brit. Mus. Add. 25,875, fol. 19 a, col. 2. (p. 36)

[102] See Bezold, Die Schatzhöhle, p. 33, and note no. 115, p. 78. (p. 36)

[103] Gen. xiv. 18-24; Heb. chap. vii. (p. 38)

[104] p. 34 'And Melchizedek was honoured by them all, and was called "Father of Kings." Because of that which the Apostle spake, "His days had no beginning, and his life no end," simple folk have imagined that he was not a man at all, and in their error have said of him that he was God. Far from it, that his days had no beginning and his life no end. For when Shem the son of Noah took him away from his parents, not a word was said how old he was when he went up from the east, nor in how many years his departure from this world took place; because he was the son of Mâlâkh, the son of Arphaxar, the son of Shem, and not the son of one of the patriarchs; for the Apostle has said that no one of his father's family ministered at the altar, and the name of his father is not written down in the genealogies, because Matthew and Luke the Evangelists wrote down the names of the patriarchs only, and hence neither the name of his father nor that of his mother are known. The Apostle then did not say that he had no parents, but only that they were not written down by Matthew and Luke in the genealogies.' Bezold, Die Schatzhöhle, p. 36; Brit. Mus. Add. 25,875, fol. 26 b, col. 1, line 22 to fol. 27 a, col. 1, line 5. In A, on fol. 39 a, a marginal note says: 'Know, O my brother readers, that in the manuscript belonging to the priest Makbal I have seen that Melchizedek's father was called Harklêîm, and his mother Shêlâthêîl (Salathiel).' (p. 38)

[105] See also Bezold, Die Schatzhöhle, p. 28. (p. 38)

[106] Genesis, chap. x. (p. 40)

[107] So always, as in the Peshîttâ, for Arphaxad. (p. 40)

[108] The Peshîttâ has 'and their dwelling was from Manshâ, which is at the entering in of mount Sepharvaïm in the east.' (p. 40)

[109] Perhaps we might read, 'Assyria to the east, and Persia, and the Great Sea on the south.' (p. 40)

[110] Gen. x. 30. In the Oxford MS. chap. xxiv begins here. (p. 40)

[111] Perhaps Solomon means the 'five kings of the Amorites,' Josh. x. 5; or else he refers to the 'seven nations,' Deut. vii. 1. (p. 40)

[112] According to Gen. x. 7, we should read Cush. (p. 40)

[113] See Gen. x. 10. Solomon's ideas as to what is meant by Erech, Accad, and Calneh are, of course, utterly erroneous. Erech is the ruins of Warkâ, on the left bank of the lower Euphrates, S.E. of Babylon; Accad is a name for Upper Babylonia, as opposed to Sumir or Lower Babylonia; Calneh has not yet been identified. See also Schrader, The Cuneiform Inscriptions and the Old Testament, p. 78. (p. 40)

¹¹⁴ Some Assyriologists consider the biblical Shinar to be the same as Sumir or Lower Babylonia. See Lenormant, Études Accad. ii. 3, p. 70. (p. 40)

¹¹⁵ It is certain that the name Babel or Babylon has no connection with the Heb. כָּלַל {Hebrew: BâLaL} or כָּלְבָל {Hebrew: BaLaBeL}; in the cuneiform inscriptions bâb-ilu means 'Gate of God,' and is the Semitic equivalent of the Akkadian ka-dingirra-ki. (p. 40)

¹¹⁶ See Hoffmann, Auszüge aus syr. Akten pers. Märtyrer, pp. 184-186. (p. 41)

¹¹⁷ Or possibly, 'and the Amnê (Emim), whom he inherited.' (p. 41)

¹¹⁸ In the Oxford MS. chap. xxv begins here. (p. 41)

¹¹⁹ For Dodanîm or Rodanîm. See Gen. x. 4. (p. 41)

¹²⁰ Genesis, chap. xi. The numbers of the years of the Patriarchs agree neither with the Hebrew nor the LXX. (p. 42)

¹²¹ In the Oxford MS. 138 years. (p. 42)

¹²² 'From Adam until that time they all spoke this language, that is to say Syriac, which is Aramean; for this language is the king of all languages. The early writers have erred, in that they say that Hebrew was the primitive language; and here have they mingled ignorant error with their writings. For all the tongues that are in the world are taken from Syriac, and all the languages in books are mixed with it.' Bezold, Die Schatzhöhle, p. 21; Brit. Mus. Add. 25,875, fol. 22 a, col. 1. (p. 42)

¹²³ Gen. xi. 20, 21, two hundred and thirty-nine. (p. 42)

¹²⁴ Gen. xi. 22, 23, two hundred and thirty. (p. 42)

¹²⁵ Gen. xi. 24, twenty-nine. (p. 42)

¹²⁶ According to the 'Cave of Treasures,' the origin of magic was this: 'In the days of Terah, in his ninetieth year, magic appeared on the earth in the city of Ur, which Horon the son of Eber had built. Now there was in it a certain man who was very rich, and he died about that time. His son made for him an image of gold, and set it up on his grave; and he put a youth to watch it. Then Satan went and dwelt in that image, and he used to speak to the young man in the form of his father. But thieves went in and stole everything which the young man possessed; and he went to his father's grave weeping. And Satan spake with him, saying, "Weep not before

me, but go, bring thy little son, and sacrifice him to me as a sacrifice; and everything which thou hast lost shall be restored to thee immediately." So he straightway did as Satan commanded him; and he slew his son, and bathed in his blood. Then Satan went forth from the image immediately, and entered into the young man, and taught him magic, incantation, divinations, chaldeeism, destinies, haps, and fates. And behold, from that time men began to sacrifice their children to demons and to worship idols, for the demons went in and dwelt in all the images. In the one hundredth year of Nahor, when God saw that men sacrificed their children to devils, and bowed down to idols, He opened the storehouses of the wind.' Bezold, Die Schatzhöle, p. 32; Brit. Mus. Add. 25,875 fol. 23 b, col. 1, line 19 to fol. 24 a, col. 1 line 2. (p. 42)

[127] Schoenfelder, custodiam spirituum et superorum! (p. 42)

[128] In the Oxford MS. 205 years. (p. 42)

[129] Read 3323 years. In the Oxford MS. 3330 years. (p. 42)

[130] I.e. the Septuagint. (p. 42)

[131] Gen. xi. (p. 44)

[132] Gen. xii and following. (p. 45)

[133] Ibn Ezra explains it by 'a cave within a cave.' (p. 45)

[134] See Job i. (p. 46)

[135] Gen. xxvii. (p. 48)

[136] The Oxford MS. omits to explain the meanings of the names of Jacob's sons. (p. 48)

[137] Dinah was the daughter of Leah, Gen. xxx. 21. (p. 48)

[138] The Oxford MS. gives 108 years. (p. 48)

[139] The Oxford MS adds that Jacob and Esau buried their father in the 'double cave.' (p. 48)

[140] Gen. xxxvii, xxxix, xli-l. (p. 49)

[141] Gen. xv. 13, Exod. xii. 40. (p. 49)

[142] Exod. ii-iv. (p. 51)

[143] I do not know the meaning of this word nor its correct pronunciation. (p. 51)

[144] Brit. Mus. MS. Or. 2441, fol. 374 a, col. 1. On the margin is written, 'When Moses was born, he was thrown into the river, and Shipôr the Egyptian, the daughter of Pharaoh, took him out.' Bezold, Die Schatzhöhle, p. 41; Brit. Mus. Add. 25,875, fol. 30 a, col. 1. (p. 51)

[145] This looks like a corruption of the Egyptian name Het-Heru-mes or Athormes, 'born of Athor.' She was also called Makrî; see note 146. (p. 51)

[146] 'And he was in the house of Pharaoh forty years, and then he slew Pethkôm the Egyptian, the chief baker of Pharaoh. When this was heard in the house of Pharaoh, after Makrî the daughter of Pharaoh--who was called the "Trumpet of Egypt," and who reared up Moses--was dead, he feared,' etc. See Bezold, Die Schatzhöhle, p, 42; Brit. Mus. Add. 25,875, fol. 30 a, col. 2. (p. 51)

[147] In the Oxford MS. chap. xxxiv begins here. (p. 54)

[148] The Oxford MS. omits this sentence. (p. 54)

[149] The Oxford MS. adds the names of the sorcerers, Jannes and Jambres. For accounts of them see 2 Timothy iii. 8; Abulpharagius, Historia Dynast., ed. Pococke, p. 17; and Fabricius, Cod. Pseud. Vet. Test., vol. i, p. 819. (p. 55)

[150] See Löw, Aramäische Pflanzennamen, p. 81. (p. 56)

[151] I.e. Elim, Exod. xv. 27. (p. 57)

[152] See Assemânî, Bibl. Or., t. iii, pt. i, pp. 49 and 99. (p. 57)

[153] C reads 'ten words.' (p. 57)

[154] The word is explained in the text by the Arabic {word for} 'indigestion.' (p. 59)

[155] Ps. cvi. 30. (p. 63)

[156] Deut. xxii. 5. (p. 64)

[157] Deut. xxii. 6. (p. 64)

[158] Deut. xxii. 7 {sic Deut. xxii. 8}. (p. 64)

[159] Deut. xxi. 18-20. (p. 64)

[160] Deut. xxi. 23. (p. 64)

[161] Lev. xxiv. 16. (p. 64)

[162] Deut. xxii. 26-29 {sic Deut. xxii. 23-25}. (p. 64)

[163] Deut. xxxi. 1-7. (p. 65)

[164] Deut. xvi. 13. (p. 65)

[165] Deut. xxxi. 14-16. (p. 65)

[166] Deut. xxxiv. 6. (p. 65)

[167] Oxford MS. 3860 years. (p. 65)

[168] Exod. xii. 37. (p. 65)

[169] Seventy souls according to Gen. xlvi. 27; Exod. i. 5; Deut. x. 22. (p. 65)

[170] Josh. i. 2-3. (p. 66)

[171] Exod. xiv. 21, 22. (p. 66)

[172] Josh. iv. 3. (p. 66)

[173] Josh. vi. 21. (p. 66)

[174] Josh. xii. 9-24. (p. 66)

[175] Syr. Adar. (p. 66)

[176] Syr. Arlam. (p. 66)

[177] Syr, Makar. (p. 66)

[178] Syr. Neshrôn. (p. 66)

[179] Syr. Shâmrîn, Samaria. (p. 66)

[180] Syr. Magdôl. (p. 66)

[181] Syr. Nekem`am or Nak`âm. (p. 66)

[182] Syr, `Umkâ. (p. 66)

[183] The Oxford MS. omits the names of these kings. (p. 66)

[184] In the Oxford MS. 'in the book of Kings.' The term ### properly includes Joshua, Judges, Samuel, Kings, Proverbs, Ecclesiasticus, Ecclesiastes, Ruth, the Song of Songs, and Job, See Wright's Catalogue, p. 103, col. 1, note †. (p. 66)

[185] Deut. xxix. 5. (p. 66)

[186] Josh. xxiv. 29. Josephus, Antiq., v. 1, gives twenty-nine years. Eusebius and Andronicus, twenty years; the Ausar Râzê (Brit. Mus. MS. Add. 21,580, fol. 69 a) twenty-seven years. (p. 66)

[187] Bar Hebraeus says that the elders of the people ruled after Joshua, but no number of years is given; his list of the Judges is much fuller, but their years do not agree with those given in this chapter. In Brit. Mus. Add. 21,580, fol. 69 a, after Joshua, there follows Chushan the wicked, eight years; Othniel, forty years; the Moabites, eighteen years; and Ahôr or Ehud comes next. (p. 66)

[188] Judg. iii. 14. The Oxford MS. has 'Og, king of the Moabites.' (p. 66)

[189] Judg. iii. 30. (p. 66)

[190] Judg. iv. 3. (p. 67)

[191] Judg. v. 31. (p. 67)

[192] Judg. vi. 1. The Oxford MS. gives seventy years. (p. 67)

[193] Judg. viii. 28. (p. 67)

[194] Solomon has here confused Abdon with Gideon; see Judg. xii. 14. (p. 67)

[195] We should probably read 'three years.' See Judg. ix. 22. (p. 67)

[196] Judg. x. 2. (p. 67)

[197] Judg. x. 3. (p. 67)

[198] Judg. x. 8. (p. 67)

[199] Judg. xii. 7. (p. 67)

[200] Judg. xii. 9. (p. 67)

[201] Judg. xii. 11. (p. 67)

[202] Judg. xii. 14. The Oxford MS. makes no mention of Abdon. (p. 67)

[203] Judg. xiii. 1. (p. 67)

[204] Judg. xv. 20. The Oxford MS. gives 'forty years.' After Samson, Brit. Mus. Add. 21,580, fol. 70 a, has 'without Judges, twelve years.' (p. 67)

[205] 1 Sam. iv. 18. (p. 67)

[206] 1 Sam. vii. 2. (p. 67)

[207] Twenty years, Brit. Mus. Add. 21,580, fol. 70 a. (p. 67)

[208] So Eusebius, but Anianus gives twenty years. (p. 67)

[209] The numbers here given amount to 642 years. (p. 67)

[210] 1 Kings ii. 11. (p. 67)

[211] 1 Kings xi. 42. (p. 67)

[212] 1 Kings xiv. 21. (p. 67)

[213] 1 Kings xv. 2. (p. 67)

[214] 1 Kings xv. 10. (p. 67)

[215] 1 Kings xxii. 42. (p. 67)

[216] 2 Kings viii. 17. Jehoram is omitted by the Oxford MS. (p. 67)

[217] 2 Kings viii. 26. (p. 67)

[218] 2 Kings xi. 3. (p. 67)

[219] 2 Kings xii. 1. Joash is omitted by the Oxford MS. (p. 67)

[220] Twenty-nine years, 2 Kings xiv. 2. (p. 67)

[221] 2 Kings xv. 2. (p. 67)

[222] 2 Kings xv. 33. Ahaz the son of Jotham also reigned sixteen years (2 Kings xvi. 2); the length of the reigns of the father and son being the same is no doubt the cause why the latter is omitted in all the MSS. (p. 67)

[223] 2 Kings xviii. 2. (p. 67)

[224] 2 Kings xxi. 1. (p. 67)

[225] 2 Kings xxi. 19. (p. 67)

[226] 2 Kings xxii. 1. (p. 67)

[227] 2 Kings xxiii. 31. (p. 67)

[228] 2 Kings xxiii. 36. (p. 67)

[229] 2 Kings xxiv. 8, 'three months.' (p. 67)

[230] 2 Kings xxiv. 18. The Oxford MS. makes no mention of Jehoiachin, and gives the name of Zedekiah without the length of his reign. (p. 67)

[231] The numbers here given amount to 451 years, 6 months, and 10 days. (p. 67)

[232] See Epiphanius, De Prophetarum Vitis, in Migne, Patrologiae Cursus, Ser. Gr., t. 43, cols. 415-427. (p. 68)

[233] Rather obscure; ### signifies 'he hid, concealed, buried;' possibly the meaning may be 'brought by an underground tunnel.' (p. 68)

[234] Schoenfelder, eum in terram projecerunt. (p. 68)

[235] Epiphanius says that Amaziah slew him. (p. 68)

[236] Solomon here follows the tradition adopted by Jerome and Ephraim Syrus, and maintained by Kimchi and Abarbanel. He is supposed to have been the captain of the third fifty of soldiers sent by Ahab against Elijah. See 2 Kings i. 13. (p. 68)

[237] Or Tishbeh. Epiphanius, 'from the land of the Arabs.' (p. 68)

[238] Elijah is called 'the son of Shôbâkh' in the Oxford MS. Epiphanius, Σοβάχ {Greek: Sobáx}. (p. 69)

[239] Epiphanius, 'the golden heifer.' (p. 69)

[240] In the Syriac, Yaunân the son of Mattai. (p. 69)

[241] Gath-hepher in the tribe of Zebulun, 2 Kings xiv. 25. (p. 69)

[242] Epiphanius, ἐκ λης Καριαθιαρύμ {Greek: ek ghs Kariaðamaoúm}. A variant has Καριαθιαρίμ {Greek: Kariaðiarím} (Kirjath-jearim). (p. 69)

[243] Or Surdânôs. See Hoffmann, Auszüge aus syr. Akten pers. Märtyrer, note 369, page 43. The only son of Sennacherib whose name can be compared with this is Assur-nadin-sumi. (p. 69)

[244] Epiphanius, Καὶ κατοικήδας ἐν γῇ Σαὰρ, ἐκεῖ ἀπέθανεν, καὶ ἐτάφη ἐν τῷ σπηλαίῳ Καινεζεοῦ {Greek: Kaì katoikhdas en gh Saàr, ekei apéðanen, kaì etáfh en tw sphlaìw Kainekseou}. (p. 69)

[245] Epiphanius attributes this prophecy to Habakkuk. (p. 69)

[246] Epiphanius, ἐξ ἀγροῦ Βηθοχήρ {Greek: eks agrou Bhðoxhr}. A variant has Βιδζεχάρ {Greek: Bidzexár}. (p. 70)

[247] See Migne, Patrologiae Cursus, Ser. Gr., t. 43, col. 421; and the chapter on the going down of our Lord into Egypt. (p. 70)

[248] Epiphanius, ἐκ γῆς Σαρηρά {Greek: ek ghs Sarhrá}. (p. 70)

[249] In Arabic al-Ahwâz, now Khûzistân. (p. 71)

[250] Epiphanius, ἐκ γῆς Συνβαθά {Greek: ek ghs Sunbaðá}. (p. 71)

[251] Bar Bahlûl (Brit. Mus. Or. 2441, fol. 343 b, col. 1) explains this word thus: 'according to Bar Sarôshwai they were two balustrades (or banisters), between

which the steps were built.' Another lexicon, Brit. Mus. Add. 7203, fol. 159 a, col. 2, says: 'the raised platform (or dais) which is before the door of the altar.' (p. 71)

[252] See Gen. v, Matt. i, and Luke iii. 23-38. (p. 72)

[253] This sentence is omitted by the Oxford MS., as well as several names from the genealogies. (p. 72)

[254] Matt. i. 6-16. (p. 72)

[255] Luke iii. 23-31. (p. 72)

[256] Joseph, Juda, and Simeon should follow here. See Luke iii. 29, 30. (p. 73)

[257] See William Hone, The Apocryphal New Testament, 8vo, London, 1820, Protevangelion and Mary; Wright, Contributions to the Apocryphal Literature of the New Testament, p. 1; Cowper, The Apocryphal Gospels, pp. 3, 29, and 84 foll.; Tischendorf, Evangelia Apocrypha, Leipzig, 1853, pp. 53 foll.; Thilo, Codex Apocryphus Novi Testamenti, Lipsiae, 1832, t. i, pp. 162 foll. For a list of other works on the Apocryphal Gospels, see Migne, Dictionnaire des Apocryphes, col. 962. (p. 74)

[258] Then her mother caught her up and said, 'As the Lord my God liveth, thou shalt not walk again on this earth till I bring thee into the temple of the Lord.' Hone, Apoc. New Test., Mary, chap. vi. 2. (p. 74)

[259] Hane, Apoc. New Test., chap. viii. 31. (p. 74)

[260] Ibid., chap. ix. (p. 75)

[261] In the MS. Niktîbûs. (p. 76)

[262] Num. v. 18. (p. 77)

[263] See Hone, Apoc. New Test., Protevangelion, chap. xi; Cowper, Apocryphal Gospels, p. 48; Thilo, Codex Apocryphus, p. 372; Tischendorf, Evangelia Apoc., p. 72. (p. 77)

[264] Luke ii. 1-2. The name is written in the MSS. of 'the Bee' Κυρῖνος {Greek: Kurinos} = Quirinus. (p. 78)

[265] The extract from the History of the Virgin runs as follows: 'When they drew near to Bethlehem, Mary said to Joseph, "The day of giving birth has come, and the

birth-pains will not allow me to reach the city; let us enter this cave, for my womb . . . ." When she had gone into the cave, Joseph ran to call a woman to be with her. And lo, while he was running, there met him an old Samaritan woman, who was travelling from Jerusalem to go to Bethlehem. Joseph said to her, "Come, O blessed matron, and go into this cave, where there is a woman giving birth to a child." When the old woman came, Joseph was mixing for her . . . . . ., and they had nothing in the cave. When they went in they saw,' etc. Some words seem to have been omitted in the MS. in the third line. See Cowper, Apoc. Gospels, p. 51; the notes in Thilo, Codex Apoc., p. 377; and Wright, Contrib. to the Apoc. Lit. of the New Test., pp. 2 and 3. In the Gospel of Pseudo-Matthew two midwives are mentioned, Zelomi and Salome; Tischendorf, Evangelia Apoc., p. 75. (p. 78)

[266] Or rather, Gushnasp. (p. 79)

[267] Or, according to another reading, shall strive with one another. (p. 79)

[268] See Eisenmenger, Entdecktes Judenthum, Theil ii, pp. 439, 440, and 905. (p. 80)

[269] Καὶ γὰρ πρὸ πολλοῦ χρόνου δοκεῖ μοι ὁ ἀδτὴρ φανῆται {Greek: Kaì gàr prò pollou xrónou dokei moi o aothr fanhtai}. See Migne's edit., vol. vii, col. 76. 'Two years before Christ was born, a star appeared to the Magi; they saw a star in the firmament of heaven which shone with a light greater than that of any other star. Within it was a maiden carrying a child with a crown upon his head.' Brit. Mus. Add. 25,875, fol. 40 a, col. 1. See Bezold, Die Schatzhöhle, p. 56. Another legend says that the star was in the shape of an eagle having within it the form of a young child, and above him the sign of the cross. Sandys, Christmas Carols, London, 1833, p. lxxxiii foll. (p. 81)

[270] The Cave of Treasures (Brit. Mus. Add. 25,875, fol. 40 b, col. 2; Bezold, Die Schatzhöhle, p. 57) gives the names of three kings only: 'Hôrmîzdâd of Mâkhôzdî, the king of Persia, who was called "king of kings" and dwelt in lower Adhôrgîn; and Izdegerd the king of Sâbâ, and Pêrôzâd the king of Shabâ in the East.' (p. 83)

[271] The Oxford MS. adds: 'They were laid in the ark, and afterwards in the land of Persia.' (p. 83)

[272] Micah v. 2. (p. 83)

[273] See Hone, Protevangelion, Infancy, chap. iii. 4-10. The passage from the History of the Virgin Mary, given in the notes, is as follows: 'And Mary took one of the swaddling bands of Jesus, and gave it to the Persian Magi, and they received it from her in faith as a sublime gift . . . . . . They held a Magian feast, and made a huge fire, and cast the swaddling band into the fire, which they worshipped; and

the swaddling band became like fire, and quenched that fire. Then they brought it out from the fire when it was like snow, even purer than at first. And they took it and kissed it and laid it upon their eyes, saying, "Verily without doubt this is the God of gods, for the fire of our god was not able to burn it or injure it." And they took it with faith and great honour.' (p. 83)

[274] See Hone, Protevangelion, chap. xvi. 9-28; Tischendorf, Evangelia Apocrypha, p. 45; Cowper, Apoc. Gospels, p. 24; Thilo, Coli Apoc., p. 265; Wright, Contributions to the Apoc. Lit. of the New Test., p. 5. (p. 84)

[275] See above, p. 71, note 251. (p. 84)

[276] See Taanîth, fol. 69, Tal. Jer., and Sanhedrîm, fol. 96, Tal. Babli. (p. 84)

[277] Matt. chap. ii. (p. 85)

[278] In the Thebaïd. For the opinions of the ancient writers on this subject see Tillemont, Mém. Eccles., i. 8. (p. 85)

[279] When Christ entered Egypt, ail the idols fell down and were broken. See Fabricius, Evangel. Infantiae, p. 175; Migne; Dict. des Apoc., vol. xxiv, p. 926; Thilo, Codex Apoc., p. 399; Cowper, Apoc. Gospels, p. 63. (p. 85)

[280] See Löw, Aram. Pflanzennamen, p. 73, no. 53. (p. 85)

[281] Matt. chap. iii. (p. 87)

[282] Μαχαιροῦς {Greek: Maxairous}, a fortress situated on the eastern shore of the Dead Sea; Josephus, Antiq., xviii. 5. 2. (p. 87)

[283] Matt. xi. 3. (p. 88)

[284] See Löw, Aram. Pflanzennamen, p. 209, no. 155. (p. 88)

[285] Σταφυλῖνος {Greek: Stafulinos}. See Löw, Aram. Pflanzennamen, p. 86, no. 64. (p. 88)

[286] Matt. chap. iv. (p. 89)

[287] Matt. chap. xxvi. (p. 90)

[288] In the Oxford MS. this chapter ends here. (p. 90)

[289] Isaiah of Scêtê. See Assemânî, Bibl. Orient., t. iii, pt. i, p. 99; Wright's Catal., p. 458 sqq., p. 868, col. 2. (p. 90)

[290] The Oxford MS. omits this sentence. (p. 92)

[291] John v. 14. The Oxford MS. adds passages from Isaiah, Zechariah and the Psalms, and after these our Lord's statement that He would rise again and restore the temple in three days. (p. 92)

[292] In the Oxford MS, the purple is said to have been made for Hiram, king of Tyre, who sent it to Solomon, and he placed it in the Sanctuary. (p. 92)

[293] In the Oxford MS. a long account of the baptism of Adam is introduced here. (p. 92)

[294] John xix. 34. See Chrysostom's Homilies on St. John's Gospel, ed. Migne, vol. viii, col. 465, lines 24-30, (p. 92)

[295] ### = δρακμή {Greek: draxmh} (p. 93)

[296] Melchior, one of the Persian Magi, offered to Christ thirty pieces of gold, which had been coined by Terah the father of Abraham. Joseph paid them into the treasury of Sheba for spices to embalm Jacob, and the queen of Sheba gave them to Solomon, Sandys, Christmas Carols, London, 1883, p, lxxxiii foll. (p. 93)

[297] In the Oxford MS. chap. xlix begins here, fol. 176 a. (p. 94)

[298] The Oxford MS. here gives an account of the taking down of our Lord from the cross, and of His burial by Joseph. (p. 94)

[299] In the Oxford MS. a new chapter begins here, fol. 177 a. (p. 94)

[300] According to the Oxford MS., 13 years. (p. 94)

[301] So also in the Oxford MS.; but in the History of the Virgin, MS. A, fol. 157 b, we read: 'And the blessed Mary departed this life in the year of Alexander three hundred and ninety-four (i.e. p. 98 A.D. 82-3). At the Annunciation she was thirty years old, and she lived also the [thirty]-three years of the Dispensation; and after the Crucifixion she lived fifty-eight years. The years which she lived were one hundred and twenty-one.' (p. 94)

[302] In the History of the Virgin, fol. 156 a, we read as follows: 'And Mary remained in Jerusalem, and grieved because of her separation from our Lord Jesus Christ,

and the absence of the apostles from her. And she prayed and cast frankincense into the fire, and lifted up her eyes and spread out her hands to heaven, and said, "O Christ, the Son of the living God, hearken unto the voice of Thy handmaiden, and send unto me Thy friend John the young with his fellow-apostles, that I may see them and be comforted by the sight of them before the day of my death; and I will praise and adore Thy goodness." And straightway it was revealed by the Holy Spirit to each one of the apostles, in whatever country he was in, that the blessed Mary was about to depart from this world into the never-ending life. And the Spirit summoned them, along with those of them who were dead, to be gathered together at daybreak to the blessed Mary for her to see them: and each one of them came to her from his own land at dawn by the agency of the Holy Spirit, and they saluted Mary and each other, and adored her.' See Wright, Contributions to the Apoc. Lit. of the New Test. (p. 94)

[303] The two following paragraphs do not appear in the Oxford MS. (p. 94)

[304] John xx. 11, 18. (p. 96)

[305] Matt. xxviii. 9, 10. (p. 96)

[306] Luke xxiv. 18. (p. 96)

[307] Luke xxiv. 34. (p. 96)

[308] Luke xxiv. 36-49; John xx. 19-23. (p. 96)

[309] John xx. 24-29. (p. 96)

[310] Matt. xxviii. 16-20. (p. 96)

[311] John xxi. 1-24. (p. 96)

[312] Mark xvi. 19; Luke xxiv. 50, 53. (p. 96)

[313] 'After that, he was seen of above five hundred brethren at once; of whom the greater part remain unto this present, but some are fallen asleep.' 1 Cor. xv. 6. (p. 96)

[314] Acts ix. 3-9; 1 Cor. xv. 8. (p. 96)

[315] Acts vii. 55-60. (p. 96)

[316] In the Oxford MS. there follows here a long discussion on the divine and human natures of Christ, in the middle of which (fol. 178 b) is a Syriac passage in which the names of Athanasius and Gregory are mentioned. The view there maintained is that Christ is God and man in the unity of one Person. (p. 97)

[317] A new chapter begins here in the Oxford MS., fol. 180 a. (p. 98)

[318] A new chapter begins here in the Oxford MS., fol. 180 b. (p. 98)

[319] See Assemânî, Bibl. Orient., t. iii, pt. i, p. 165. (p. 98)

[320] See Assemânî, Bibl. Orient., t. iii, pt. i, pp. 239, 241, 358, and 608. (p. 99)

[321] See the lives of the apostles and disciples by Pseudo-Dorotheus, edited by Du Cange in the Chronicon Paschale, Paris, 1868, p. 164; Hanmer, Eusebius, pp. 532 foll., London, 1636; Cave, Lives of the Apostles, Cary's ed., Oxford, 1840; Pseudo-Epiphanius, De Prophetis, eorumque obitu ac sepultura, Migne, Patrologiae p. 104 Ser. Gr., vol. 43, col. 393 foll.; Tillemont, Mémoires pour servir à l'histoire ecclés., Paris, 1701, 4to; Lipsius, Die Apokryphen Apostelgeschichten, Braunschweig, 1884; and Brit. Mus. Add. 14,601, fol. 163 b. (p. 101)

[322] The Nestorian Fast of the Apostles begins on Whit-Monday and ends on June 29th. See Badger, The Nestorians and their Rituals, vol. ii, p. 188; Assemânî, Bibl. Orient., t. iii, pt. i, p. 501. (p. 101)

[323] The orthodox Christians, who accept the doctrines on the natures of our Lord as laid down by the Council of Chalcedon. For the origin of the name, etc., see Renaudot, Historia Patriarcharum Alexandrinorum Jacobitarum, p. 119; and Assemânî, Bibl. Orient., t. i, p. 507; t. iii, pt. i, p. 354, col. 2. (p. 101)

[324] See Butler, Lives of the Saints, vol. ii, Dec. 27. (p. 101)

[325] This sentence is omitted by the Oxford MS. Dorotheus and Pseudo-Epiphanius say that he was bnried in Judaea, though some MSS. of the former have ἐν πόλει τῆς Μαρμαρικῆς {Greek: en pólei ths Marmarikhs}, the original of the Latin 'in arce Marmarica.' Μαρμαρική {Greek: Marmarikh} is the most eastern land of N. Africa. Isidore of Seville says: 'Jacobus filius Zebedaei frater Joannis quartus in ordine. Hispaniae et occidentalibus locis evangelium praedicavit et in occasum mundi lucem praedicationis infudit. Hic ab Herode tetrarcha gladio caesus occubuit sepultus in Azimarmaria [arce marmaria].' See Lipsius, Apostelgeschichten, ii. 2, pp. 208, 209, and 214, note 1; Acta Sanctorum, vol. xxxiii, July 25; Tillemont, Mémoires, p. 512. (p. 102)

[326] See Acta Sanctorum, vol. xiv, May 1; Lipsius, Apostelgeschichten, ii. 2, p. 26. (p. 102)

[327] Oxford MS. in India and Sind and Persia. (p. 102)

[328] See Wright, Apoc. Acts, vol. ii, p. 297; Acta Thomae, ed. M. Bonnet, p. 83 sqq.; Lipsius, Apostelgeschichten, i, p. 236. (p. 102)

[329] See Assemânî, Bibl. Orient., t. i, pp. 49, 399, and 403; Socrates, Hist. Eccles., iv. 18; Bar-Hebraeus, Chron. Eccles., ed. Abbeloos and Lamy, i. 31, and iii. 4 foll. (p. 102)

[330] The Oxford MS. says that he was buried in India. See Lipsius, Apostelgeschichten, i, p. 246; Butler, Lives of the Saints, Dec. 21. (p. 102)

[331] al-Jabbûl, a town in Coelesyria. (p. 102)

[332] See Tillemont, Mémoires, i, pp. 391 foll.; Acta Sanctorum, xlviii, Sept. 21; Lipsius, Apostelgeschichten, ii. 2, p. 127. (p. 102)

[333] According to the Armenian Acts of Bartholomew (Lipsius, Apostelgeschichten, ii. 2, p. 94), he went first to Golthon in Armenia, and, in the 29th year of Sanatruk came back to the hill Artaschu; he next went to Her and Zarevant, and afterwards to Urbianos, where he was martyred. (p. 102)

[334] {Ketarbôl} was a place between Baghdâd and `Ukbarâ, celebrated for its wine; but this can hardly come into account. (p. 102)

[335] According to other MSS., Rhûstnî or Hêrôstnî. The king of Armenia in the time of Bartholomew was called Sanadrog (Sanatruk). Florival, Moïse de Khorène, ii, p. 233. See also Lipsius, Apostelgeschichten, ii. 2, pp. 59, 99, and 104; and Acta Sanctorum, xxxix, Aug. 24. (p. 102)

[336] The latter name is more correctly Ruwâd. Antaradus is now called Antartûs. (p. 102)

[337] See Lipsius, Apostelgeschichten, ii. 2, pp. 142-200; and Acta Sanctorum, lx, Oct. 28. (p. 102)

[338] See Lipsius, Apostelgeschichten, ii. 2, p. 147; Acta Sanctorum, lx, Oct. 28. (p. 102)

[339] See Lipsius, Apostelgeschichten, ii. 2, pp. 229-257; Acta Sanctorum, xiv, May 1. (p. 103)

[340] See Lipsius, Apostelgeschichten, ii. 2, pp. 258-269. (p. 103)

[341] See Lipsius, Apostelgeschichten, ii, 2, p. 231; Acta Sanctorum, xiv, May 1. (p. 103)

[342] So we read instead of Arîl, following the Oxford MS. Solomon was probably copying from an Arabic MS., in which the difference would be very slight. (p. 103)

[343] The MS. C has Aristus. (p. 103)

[344] The MS. A has: Paul of Tarsus was of the tribe of Benjamin; he was a Pharisee by sect. (p. 103)

[345] Reading in the plural with the MS. B. (p. 103)

[346] See Acta Sanctorum, xxvii, June 30. (p. 104)

[347] Oxford MS., Aleppo. (p. 104)

[348] See Lipsius, Apostelgeschichten, ii. 2, pp. 356-360; Acta Sanctorum, lvi, Oct. 18. (p. 104)

[349] See Lipsius, Apostelgeschichten, ii. 2, pp. 323-325; Acta Sanctorum, xii, April 25. (p. 104)

[350] In Brit. Mus. Add. 14,601, fol. 164 a, col. 1, line 17, he is called Severus. (p. 104)

[351] Egil, or Engil, ###, Ἀγγιληνή {Greek: 'Aggilhnh}, north of Âmid. (p. 104)

[352] See The Doctrine of Addai, ed. Phillips, p. 49. (p. 104)

[353] The Oxford MS. gives the name of this martyr only: a blank space has been left in it for about eight lines. (p. 105)

[354] The Oxford MS. says that when the crucifiers knew that Nicodemus had become a Christian, they seized his property and slew him; and that his brother Gamaliel buried him in Kephar Gamlâ. It then gives the following account of Gamaliel. Gamaliel was a friend of the crucifying Jews, but was afterwards baptised together with his son: he lived for twenty years after this. When they died, they were buried by the side of Nicodemus in Kephar Gamlâ, where Stephen was buried.

Many years after (about A.D. 415), God revealed their place of burial to one of the saints (Lucian), and they sought for the remains of the bodies by digging, and found them; and there they built a church. Foll. 187 b, 188 a. See also Migne, Biog. Chrét., ii. 73; Wright, Cat. Syr. MSS., iii, p. 1047, i. 8. (p. 105)

[355] Oxford MS. in the mount of Hebron, the city of David. (p. 105)

[356] Galat. ii. 9; 1 Cor. i. 12. For a discussion of the identity of this Cephas with Simon Peter, see P. M. Molkenbuhr, Dissertatio script. crit. An Cephas . . . fuerit Simon Petrus, 4to, 1785. (p. 105)

[357] Oxford MS. He preached the Gospel to the people of Baalbek, Hims and Batharûn, and taught the people of Sarmîn; he was buried at Kurâmah (?). Sarmîn approaches the reading of B, C; it is in the district of Aleppo. Shirâz is perhaps a mistake for Shaizar. (p. 105)

[358] The Oxford MS., like B and C, makes no mention of Barnabas. See also Lipsius, Apostelgeschichten, ii. 2, pp. 270-320; Acta Sanctorum, xxii, June 11. (p. 105)

[359] See Lipsius, Apostelgeschichten, ii. 2, pp. 401-406; Acta Sanctorum, i, Jan. 4. (p. 105)

[360] The Oxford and Vatican MSS., as well as B and C, make no mention of Narcissus. (p. 106)

[361] The Arabic name is Ahwâz. Oxford MS., `Irâk. (p. 106)

[362] The Vatican MS. omits Onesimus. (p. 106)

[363] A has Luke. (p. 106)

[364] Vat. MS. Linus. (p. 107)

[365] The Vat. MS. omits Silas. (p. 107)

[366] The Oxford MS. omits Jason. (p. 107)

[367] The Vat. MS. omits these names. (p. 107)

[368] The Vat. MS. omits this name. (p. 107)

[369] The Oxford MS. makes no mention of this martyr. (p. 107)

[370] See Matt. x, Mark iii, Luke vii, Acts i; and Pseudo-Dorotheus, Migne, Dict. des Apocr., vol. ii, p. 207. (p. 109)

[371] See Assemânî, Bibl. Orient., iii, pt. i, pp. 319-320, where lists of the twelve apostles and seventy disciples are given from the Vatican MS. of the Book of the Bee, from the Commentary of Bar-Hebraeus on St. Matthew, and from the Synopsis of ʿAmr and Mâri, etc. (p. 109)

[372] Acts xvii. 5-9. (p. 109)

[373] The Oxford MS. omits Rufus. Rom. xvi. 13. (p. 109)

[374] So all the MSS., but ten names follow, or eleven, if we read Andronicus, Junias, Titus. (p. 109)

[375] In Acts xxi. 9, Philip is said to have had four daughters. The Oxford MS. reads four. (p. 109)

[376] Acts vi. 5. (p. 109)

[377] Rom. xvi. 7. (p. 109)

[378] Seven names follow in all the MSS. (p. 109)

[379] 2 Tim. iv. 10. The Oxford MS. omits Criscus and Gaius. (p. 109)

[380] See 1 John ii. 19. Solomon is mistaken as to the author of these words. (p. 109)

[381] 2 Cor. xi. 13. (p. 109)

[382] Oxford MS. Alexander. (p. 109)

[383] Oxford MS. Paul. (p. 110)

[384] Matt. xviii. 2. See Nicephorus, Hist., bk. ii, chap. iii. (p. 111)

[385] Socrates, Eccles. Hist., chap. viii. (p. 111)

[386] Assemânî thinks that this embassy is a mistake on the part of Solomon, arising from his having misunderstood a pasage in Theodoret, Hist. Eccles., lib. 2, cap. xxiv. See Bibl. Orient., t. iii, pt. i, p. 321. (p. 111)

[387] Compare the lists in Assemânî, Bibl. Orient., t. ii, pp. 387-392. For the lives of the Catholics of the East, see ibid., pp. 391-457. (p. 112)

[388] In Arabic Dair Kunnâ; 16 parasangs from Baghdâd, on the left bank of the Tigris, a mile from the river. See Yâkût in the Mu`jam al-Buldân; Abbeloos, Acta S. Maris, index. (p. 112)

[389] Be`esh-shemîn for Be`êl-shemîn. (p. 112)

[390] See Assemânî, Bibl. Orient., t. iii, pt. i, p. 369, col. 2. (p. 113)

[391] Hêrtâ or Hîrtâ, the Hîrah of the Arabs. (p. 113)

[392] The later Arabic name for Ctesiphon. (p. 113)

[393] A place in the south or south-east part of the diocese of Bêth-Nûhâdrê, near Balad and opposite to Eski-Mosul. See Assemânî, Bibl. Orient., t. iii, pt. i, p. 477, col. 2; and Hoffmann, Auszüge aus syr. Akten pers. Märtyrer, pp. 211-212, notes 1674 and foll. (p. 113)

[394] Ἀρζανηνή {Greek: 'Arzanhnh} was a town and province of Armenia on the borders of Mesopotamia, north of Hisn Kaifâ. Schoenfelder, p. 84, writes 'Jesujab mysticus!' (p. 113)

[395] Judâl, near Mosul. (p. 113)

[396] In Syriac Hedaiyab, the district of which Arbêl or Irbil is the chief town. (p. 113)

[397] The famous convent of Bêth-`Âbê was situated in the diocese of Margâ not far from the right bank of the Great Zâb. See Hoffmann, Auszüge, p. 226, note 1798. (p. 113)

[398] Or Henân-îshô`. (p. 114)

[399] Or Theodosius. (p. 114)

[400] Dârtâ-de-Rômâyê, 'the house of the Romans' (the Byzantine Greeks), the seat of the Nestorian patriarchs at Baghdâd. See Assemânî, Bibl. Orient., t. ii, pp. 439, 440, 450. (p. 114)

[401] Assemânî, Ἰωάννης {Greek: 'Iwánnhs}; otherwise our writer commonly uses Yohannân for John. (p. 114)

[402] See note 401 on preceding page. (p. 115)

[403] The MS. A has in ʿAtîkah, or 'the old (Town),' a quarter of Baghdâd on the east or left side of the Tigris. (p. 115)

[404] This is from A alone, but correct. (p. 115)

[405] See Assemânî, Bibl. Orient., t. ii, p. 456. (p. 116)

[406] According to Assemânî, t. ii, p. 457, col. 1, Bibl. Orient., t. iii, pt. i, p. 621, col. 1, he was ordained Catholicus in 1504. The list has therefore been continued by the scribes of the different MSS. long after Solomon's time. (p. 116)

[407] See Lepsius, Königsbuch, Synoptische Tafeln, p. 9. (p. 117)

[408] The MSS. have 'the son of Philadelphus,' both here and below. (p. 117)

[409] According to Bar-Hebraeus it was in his sixth year; Chron. Syr., ed. Bruns, p. 41. A list of the 72 translators is given in Brit. Mus. Add. 14,601, fol. 162 a. See Wright, Cat. Syr. MSS., p. 792, 15 a. (p. 117)

[410] Vatican MS. Datis. (p. 117)

[411] Brit. Mus. Add. 14,601, fol. 162 a, col. 2, and Vatican MS. Jonathan. (p. 117)

[412] Brit. Mus. Add. 14,601, fol. 162 a, col. 2, and Vatican MS. Shalmî. (p. 117)

[413] Brit. Mus. Add. 14,601 wrongly, ###. The Vatican MS. has also Jonathan. (p. 117) 414 Or, as pointed in the text, Abbâyâ. (p. 118)

[415] Lepsius, 25 years. (p. 118)

[416] I.e. Ptolemy Soter II. Lepsius, 36 years. (p. 118)

[417] See the notes in Lepsius, p. 9 of the Tables. (p. 118)

[418] Lepsius, 29 years. (p. 118)

[419] For the authorities and their opinions on tbis subject, see Clinton, Fasti Hellenici, vol. iii, p. 260. (p. 118)

⁴²⁰ For the various opinions on this subject, see Clinton, Fasti Romani, vol. i, p. 12. (p. 118)

⁴²¹ He reigned 19 years (A.D. 99-117). Solomon probably includes the reign of Nerva, 1 year. (p. 119)

⁴²² He reigned 23 years (A.D. 139-161). (p. 119)

⁴²³ See Clinton, Fasti Romani, vol. i, p. 846. (p. 119)

⁴²⁴ He reigned 12 years (A.D. 181-192). (p. 119)

⁴²⁵ He reigned 18 years (A.D. 194-211). (p. 119)

⁴²⁶ Philip reigned A.D. 245-249, i.e. 5 years. Decius came next and reigned 2 years. Gallus reigned 1 year, A.D. 252. (p. 119)

⁴²⁷ Claudius reigned 2 years, A.D. 269-270; and Tacitus died A.D. 276. (p. 119)

⁴²⁸ He reigned 31 years, A.D. 307-337. (p. 119)

⁴²⁹ For a list of the Sasanian kings see Nöldeke, Geschichte der Perser und Araber sur Zeit der Sasaniden, p. 436 a; and Marsden, Numismata Orzentalia, pt. i, p. 437. (p. 119)

⁴³⁰ Schoenfelder, p. 86, quo hoc genus expirat! See Nöldeke, Geschichte der Perser und Araber, pp. 239, 290 sqq.; Assemânî, Bibl. Orient., t. ii, p. 62. (p. 120)

⁴³¹ I.e. A.D. 604. Nöldeke, Geschichte der Perser und Araber, p. 436 a. (p. 120)

⁴³² I can only make 5265 years. (p. 120)

⁴³³ It should be 'in the year 538,' as the Sasanian dynasty was founded by Ardashîr I in A.D. 226. (p. 121)

⁴³⁴ See Assemânî, Bibl. Orient., t. iii, pt. i, p. 53; and the revelation to Methodius in prison, edited by Brant, Basel, 1516, 4to, pp. 1-80. (p. 122)

⁴³⁵ Solomon has made a slip here: Methodius was bishop of Olympus and Tyre, but never of Rome. (p. 122)

⁴³⁶ Rom. i. 26, 27. (p. 122)

[437] Isa. iv. 1. (p. 123)

[438] C, Eshkîn. (p. 125)

[439] B, Dîfâr. (p. 125)

[440] C, Lûdâyê; A omits the name. (p. 125)

[441] B, Tuklâyê. (p. 125)

[442] A, C have: Kaukebâyê, Emrartâ, Garmîdô`, Cannibals, Dog-men (Cynocephali). (p. 125)

[443] B, Dunkâyê. (p. 125)

[444] B, Saltâyê.--Some of these names are biblical, e. g. Gog, Magog, and Ashkenaz. Of the others many are doubtless corrupt, as the variants shew, but a few are easily recognisable; e.g. Paktâyê, the people of Παкτύη {Greek: Paktuh} in the Thracian Chersonesus; Humnâyê = Hunnâyê, the Huns, Οὖννοι {Greek: Ounnoi}; Therkâyê, the Thracians, Θρᾷκες {Greek: Đrakes} and Âlânâyê, the Alani, 'Αλανοί {Greek: 'Alanoí}. (p. 125)

[445] The text has weasels, glossed by cats. (p. 126)

[446] See Migne, Dict. des Apoc., ii, col. 618. (p. 127)

[447] Matt. xi. 21. (p. 127)

[448] Ps. lxviii. 31. (p. 127)

[449] 1 Sam. xxvi. 10. (p. 129)

[450] See Assemânî, Bibl. Orient., t. iii, pt. i, pp. 322-323. (p. 130)

[451] Matt. xxv. 6. (p. 131)

[452] Solomon is quoting 1 Thes. iv. 15 (Peshîttâ). (p. 131)

[453] 1 Cor. xv. 51. (p. 131)

[454] 2 Cor. xii. 2. (p. 132)

[455] 1 Cor. xv. 52. (p. 132)

[456] Probably Theodore of Mopsuestia. (p. 132)

[457] See Assemânî, Bibl. Orient.; t. iii, pt. i, p. 147; Hoffmann, Opusc. Nest., p. xxi. (p. 132)

[458] 1 Cor. xv. 44. (p. 134)

[459] 1 Cor. xv. 41, 43. (p. 137)

[460] See Assemânî, Bibl. Orient., t. iii, pt. i, p. 29, and note 2. (p. 139)

[461] This sentence seems to me to be untranslatable as it now stands. (p. 139)

[462] Matt. xxv. 46. (p. 139)

[463] John xiii. 8. (p. 139)

[464] Isa. xiii. 20 (p. 140)

www.ingramcontent.com/pod-product-compliance
Lightning Source LLC
Chambersburg PA
CBHW051605010526
44119CB00056B/794